Been There, Done That

Been There, Done That

My Eventful Continental Lifetime Journey

RACHI NGAINE

Been There, Done That
2ND VERSION

Printed in the United States of America

ISBN 978-1-95843-435-2 (hc)
ISBN 978-1-958434-32-1 (sc)
ISBN 978-1-958434-33-8 (e)

Library of Congress Control Number: 2022901992

Religion/Self-Help
2022.08.26

MainSpring Books
5901 W. Century Blvd
Suite 750
Los Angeles, CA, US, 90045

www.mainspringbooks.com

Table of Contents

I dedicate this book to my late parents, David and Grace Ngaine, for raising me and my other five siblings to adulthood sacrificially with meager resources, for teaching me the real meaning of love, the essence of responsibility, accountability, the substance of integrity, a sense of belonging, the spirit of perseverance, self-esteem, and the value of caring and sharing.

Foreword

By Jennifer W. Ngaine

I am the second child in my immediate family's tree. Following graduation from high school, soon thereafter, I got employment with the World Bank as a program analyst. As a full-time employee for the bank, I enrolled in a diploma program and studied journalism. My dad had already demonstrated to me and my siblings that academic and/or professional achievements were personal gratifications. He reiterated that the driving force was the opportunity to get started, and once you start, keep going till you complete the race.

In real life, Dad completed his college studies including certification as a CPA while working full time and taking care of us.

Except missing him during dinners and other fraternities, he was present when it mattered. He always made us laugh whenever he recited events and circumstances relative to his past life. The narratives made me feel so refreshed and encouraged. My simple advice to Dad was, "Record all these stories as a 'family legacy' book so that those who read it might be turned around." Dad, you have changed me in many ways, and I am so proud of you!

You can do it by exploiting your fullest potential—despite pain, afflictions, and hurdles.

Acknowledgments

I kept on hearing this proverb: "Whenever there is will, there is a way." I didn't quite understand the actual meaning of the word *willpower* until the opportunity struck. Webster's Dictionary defines *willpower* as "the ability to control oneself, energetic determination, or exercise of creative power."

The stories in this book reflect decades of deep thought processes in my life. Overall, I benefited from an unlimited pool of in-kind resources and opportunities. People are everything in life. I tapped on and commingled with the world's heterogeneous peoples. Since I was fifteen, I had access to people from all walks of life—young, old, male, female, foreign, or countrymen. I learned that nature and humanity take effect when people with different strengths and weaknesses try to solve problems together without regard to ones' status, class, or ethnicity. I want to thank everyone for numerous ways, both past and present, for contributing to the facts in this book.

Also, volumes of voices have spoken into my life for longer periods including, family members, friends, teachers, associates, colleagues, faculty, staff, neighbors, admirers, and former students who all add up to the list of inspirers. I am deeply indebted to them for their trust and patience in anticipation of a finished product.

I appreciate the financial support that donors have sacrificed. It is probable that without such support, the stories in this book could not have been published.

Thanks to my wife and children for putting up with me in ways that no one could have tolerated. Perseverance, sacrifices, and understanding were so apparent on their part.

I express special thanks to Dr. Symon Manyara—my friend, associate, and brother—for decades of mutual support. Symon tirelessly edited the entire manuscript for style, grammar, and theme.

I thank him for his recommendations of changes in each chapter including constructive critique. I am indeed thankful to my Lord and Savior Jesus Christ, who has reconciled and coordinated the thought processes for His honor and glory and for the gracious gift of sound mind, body, and spiritual strengths. Amen.

Lastly, I reckon that the readers would identify errors, omissions, misinterpretations, misstatements, and even confusion. If so, please bear with me. To error is human, and remember, we learn from mistakes!

Special Contributions

Heartfelt thanks go to those people behind the scenes, for without their support and encouragements, this book would not have materialized.

My wife, parents, uncles, aunts, siblings, children, nephews and nieces, grandchildren, friends, neighbors, colleagues, mentors, and associates.

Finally, glory be to God, my Lord and Savior Jesus Christ, who gave me the wisdom, strength, and the opportunity to get the act in motion and for abiding with me the whole time.

Introduction
By Brother Rachi

Upon birth, my parents named me Kaaria. They named me after a namesake uncle on the father's side who was an honorable senior clan member/judge and a mentor to my father. Typically, my tribal culture (Meru) and ancestral traditions allow the firstborn son or daughter of a family to be named after the father's relatives and then the mother's relatives on successive basis. The origin of *Kaaria* is the Kenyan language.

The name means "a wise, soft-spoken man; one who speaks softly but with wisdom." People with the name Kaaria have a deep inner desire to be creative, expressive of ideas, and are opinionated.

Most African names are directly connected to a meaning.

My nephews and nieces call me "Uncle Best"; grandchildren call me "Ithe" or "Shosh"; age-mates, siblings, cousins, and Christian brethren call me brother. *Rachi* means "affable." Naturally, I am outgoing (extrovert), talkative, sociable, opinionated, open, honest, passionate, and faithful about what I believe in. I love nature, especially people, and the animal kingdom. I find myself learning as much as I could about the subject matter about anything that is of interest to me. In fact, I have read avidly about history, politics, civilizations, civil wars, human intelligence, evolution of mankind, economic systems, the English language, other languages and cultures, religion, sociology, psychology, contemporary matters, and, of course, books, which have taught me about God and the human nature.

My wife of over fifty years and I love having spiritual devotions, shopping, and special times together. We have raised four adult children, and I think it's the hardest but most rewarding joint project we have ever accomplished as a team. They came first while we ranked second. We adore them including the six grandkids and one great granddaughter. This is my first major book that I have written, but I plan to write more, Lord willing. Our family loves to walk, cook, bake, barbecue, feed people, socialize, and have fun inviting folks over for tea, prayers, Bible study, cookouts, and open-forum conversations.

I hate cruelty to humans especially children and the poor, crime, hooliganism, wickedness, corruption, and all forms of discriminations and bigotry.

Academically, I have earned an associate degree in business administration (ABA), a bachelor of business administration (BBA) in accounting degree, a master of science in professional accounting (MSPA), and I am professionally qualified both as a certified public accountant (CPA) and a chartered global management accountant (CGMA). I am retired from active accounting practice and college professorship.

As a professor, I was passionate about business and entrepreneurship. I was positive and intentional about converting business, especially accounting majors, to professional accountants and entrepreneurs.

My borrowed motto of "Never, never ever surrender!" is my lifetime story about accomplishments, failures, experiences, challenges, disappointments, fascinations, beliefs, thoughts, and hopes.

Socially, I am uncomfortable with poverty, foolishness, ignorance, illiteracy, dormancy, token infrastructures, and lack of sensitivity. Writers/composers realize that writing is a special gift/talent.

It requires opportunity, timing, resources, partners, encouragement, research, data, and a collection of facts, recollections, application, and linkages. I shared that phenomenon during a social exchange centered on personal experiences with one of my colleagues in 2007 when my colleague remarked, "Rachi, do you know what you just shared with me could be a great legacy for your family?"

I responded by saying, "Really?" The colleague's view reminded me of my wife's and our second daughter's (Jennifer) persistence. Both had always thought that my lifetime stories were funny, ideal, engaging, motivating, and could make an interesting legacy for the family and a myriad of readers.

Finally, my colleague advised me that whenever I got blessed with time and opportunity, I should make my story public and reiterated that "you owe it to your family."

Subsequently, I was reminded of Gideon's rare encounter with an angel of God in the book of Judges 6:11–23. "The Lord is with you Mighty Warrior," said the angel of the Lord to Gideon, son of Joash of the tribe of Manasseh. Again, the angel of the Lord said, "Go in with the strength you have and save Israel out of Midian's hand, I will be with you."

Gideon insisted on being given a sign that it was God talking to him. When the angel of God accepted an offering of goat meat and the unleavened bread by setting it into smoke and told Gideon to go in peace, Gideon exclaimed, "Alas, sovereign Lord! I have seen the angel of the Lord face to face!"

The Lord God replied, "Peace! Do not be afraid. You are going to live." With God's help, Gideon won battles and judged Israelis peacefully for forty years.

Up until that time, I was looking for signs that the Lord was with me to give the courage and that I had the strength and the peace of mind with ample time to get the "family legacy project named *Been There—Done That*, facts of a lifetime story," up and running.

When I disclosed to the family the intent to start writing layers of my life story bit by bit, they unanimously applauded, "It's about time!"

Well, the Lord has spoken, and there it is—almost fifteen years of facts gathering and the finished composition of jot downs. Having experienced seventy-seven years of a mixed grill of active past life, I am telling the world what it was like, how it was, what it has been like, and what the future might hold. So here I go on a long stretch of compiling an additional layer of the Ngaines' "family legacy." Praise be to God!

PART 1

Growing Up in Kenya

Early Childhood

My roots originated in Kenya, East Africa. I was born and raised in a small village called Kiangua within Meru County in the Republic of Kenya. I am the thirdborn and second son to Ngaine and Ciomutua Ngaine Mbae. They were a modest peasant couple when they started the family. My late older brother, Kaboria, died prematurely at infancy while my older sister, Eunice, passed to glory at age seventy, and then the brother that followed me rested at age seventy-one. Due to lack of affordable health care, some strange illnesses claimed their lives untimely. We thank God that they had accepted Jesus Christ as the Lord and Savior of their souls. Myself and three siblings; two sisters and our youngest brother now 71, are still living.

My parents had grown in different villages but did not know one another until adulthood. According to their own accounts, my father spent most of his childhood as an orphan. Because of severe famine caused by drought about early 1912, my grandmother returned to her family when she lost her husband (my grandfather) to the famine. While there, the famine worsened and took her life as well.

Apparently, my father became a victim of circumstances and lived among his cousins (his uncle's children) until adulthood. He retraced his roots and rejoined his tribesmen as a young warrior. On the other hand, my mother had spent most of her childhood life as a single mother's child and lived with her uncles on the father's side. Her father had become a victim of food poisoning during the famine.

Having survived the calamities of famine, economic hardships, and succeeded in related hurdles of traditional rituals and attained adulthood, they met in a community folk-song festival for the first time, where both were star dancers. They got acquainted easily and developed a lasting relationship. Neither of the parents was raised as Christians. However, while grandparents, they found their Christian faith, got converted, and were baptized David and Grace, respectively.

They lived together as husband and wife for sixty years until death separated them in 1989. Dad was eighty-three when pneumonia took him out of active life. Mom held on as a widow for an additional twenty-four years and fully retired from earthly life in 2013 at age 105 years young when she joined the saints. All of the siblings contributed mutual support. Kiangua village lies in the northeastern slopes of the renown Mount Kenya and on the western part of Meru County, a component of Eastern Province in the Republic of Kenya in East Africa. The altitude is approximately 5,500 feet above the sea.

The Meru, Amiiru are a Bantu ethnic group. They inhabit the Meru region of Kenya on the fertile lands of north and eastern slopes of Mount Kenya, in the former Eastern Province of Kenya. The name Meru refers to both people and the region, which for years was the lone administrative unit. Around 1992, the Greater Meru was subdivided into three administrative units, namely Meru Central, Nyambene; Meru South, Tharaka; and Nithi. The Greater Meru covered roughly 13,000 kilometers (5,000 square miles) stretching from the Thuci river, on the border with Embu County in the east, to the border with Isiolo County in the north.

Meru ranks in the top ten population-wise out of fifty-three Kenyan indigenous tribes. The Meru people share and maintain a staunch ritual, culture, traditions, customs, and societal values.

Identical cultural values are traceable to Embu, Kamba, Kalenjin, Kikuyu, Kipsigis, Kisii, Kuria, Luhias (some), Maasai, Muslims, and Samburu tribes. Up until the early fifties, the Merus cherished circumcision rituals (genital cleansing) for both male and female youngsters aged twelve years or older. First, the goal was—and still is, in some sectors—to deter the birth of offsprings by uncleansed pairs who venture into early sex life following puberty. Such offsprings were considered a taboo in the society. In addition, the exercise limited the leisure sexual urge on the women except for childbearing purposes while giving men sexual prowess. Research has proven that partnering women have attested to that fact. Second, although the so-called urban "modern" society is weakening many of the bonds, tribal rituals and customs still hold firm in the villages and in the more remote areas. Although each tribe naturally has its own individual rituals and customs, some aspects of tribal life can be viewed differently given that each tribal group may modify certain aspects of the status quo.

Nowadays, among Central and Eastern Kenya, female circumcision is less frequent than that of male. Male tribal rituals are annual. Male circumcision has always been considered a necessary rite of passage into adulthood. The young men are divided into age groups called Nduki. Among themselves, they choose their own leader who will, henceforth, be their delegate at tribal meetings and events. Each Nduki then chooses a distinguishing characteristic that will symbolize the group. This could be a special song like *authi* or a dance like *kaajo* or an outfit they will commonly wear (i.e., anything that will uniquely identify that particular age group). Also, instead of calling each other by real name, code names such as Baete, Baicu, Iiru, Kaajia, Mutaane, Wachia, and the likes are commonly used.

The plural name for a group of three or more is simply *ataane* or "guys" like in America.

Common to other Bantu tribes in Africa, the Meru tribe has a council of elders (*Njuri Ncheke*) called *kiama* or a judicial court which sits in overall judgment over universal clans judging, solving problems and disputes, and clarifying processes, including misunderstandings.

The Njuri Ncheke is at par to form a secret council that would deliberate on sensitive tribal matters or discipline.

Up until early 1950s when the Colonial rule declared women circumcision in Kenya illegal, marriage within members of the Meru tribe was only between circumcised couples. Any other form of union was not recognized. Children born out of wedlock did not exist, and if they did, they were kept in top secrets and given freely to couples who could not have children naturally for adoption. Cases of illegitimate children were shameful and demoralizing to a particular family and were avoided at all costs. When such matters became public, the offending teenager, especially girls, ended up becoming second or third wives to a non-related elderly member of the society.

Polygamy is legal in Kenya. In addition, the Merus mutilated the ears of all domestic animals. The belief was that such rituals, pouring and sprinkling of the infant blood, will provide overall immunity to the animals and permit longevity and productivity.

Prior to Christianity era, adults too pierced and cut an extended hole on both ears (*Guturwa matu*). Also, adults had two of the lower front healthy teeth uprooted (*Ki-inga*) for beauty and demonstration of individual courage. Trees and plants were also trimmed to allow productivity, strength, and shape. Unlike the modern infant circumcision that is performed in hospitals today, village circumcision was and is ceremonial and traditional. It is a seasonal and solemn event recognized and endeared by the community at large. Narratives of procedural details of cutting and healing are quite chilling, and, hence, I will limit the event to briefs. The detailed narratives could be scary and nerve-racking. Watch me test the odds in the latter pages (initiation to manhood).

Date of Birth Controversy

Personally, I must confess that I do not know which year, month, or day I was born. My birth was never recorded in the official Kenyan database until January 1960 when I started my first job. I have relied solely on hearsay regarding my age. My mom gave birth to six (6) children in the village with the assistance of volunteer community midwives of whom she was a member, but none of the births were recorded. The midwives had no formal training, and they could not read or write. Our baby brother was born in 1951, and I became a witness even without recalling the date and month. I had third grade education at the time, so that helped. My mother played the lead role when it was her turn to help in these communal roles.

Available records show that the first hospital maternity wing opened at Chogoria Hospital in the late 1940s. However, a rumor had circulated soon thereafter that if a child was born abnormal, the child got eliminated without the consent of the parents. Furthermore, the hospital did not have a prenatal care service, and so expectant mothers never had a clue of what they were carrying until they gave birth. As you can imagine, the scary rumor kept the village mothers aloof. C-sections were unheard of. When I was born, Kenya was under Colonial rule. Births of children born in villages were never officially recorded because it was not required, and most people were illiterate. The first area primary school had started in 1946 half a mile away from our home. By God's grace, all six of my siblings were delivered at home; two brothers and two sisters are still alive. Our older sister was claimed by pneumonia while the brother that followed me was a victim of a heart attack several years ago. My late sister was three years my senior and late brother two years my junior. Based on the available word of mouth from those that were present at my time of birth, I estimated that I was born in 1942, just for the heck of it; I just had to start somewhere to have a birth record, you see. When I gave that same information to obtain my first Kenyan identification card then called *kipande* in 1960, indicating that I was eighteen years, the registration officer concurred. He simply considered I had spent eighteen years (18) schooling minus then current year, 1960, which gave an easy 1942 as the year of birth. Thus, in the absence of the birth certificate, I got an ID card that only required the year of birth. The error of estimation is roughly plus/minus three. I am convinced that I was born earlier than 1942. This fact can be supported by the ID cards of my agemates in the village which show that in 2018, the majority of them (nine out of thirteen) were in their late seventies and early eighties.

My younger brother's ID card (another guesswork) showed he was born in 1943, which, compared to mine in 1942, reflects that we were born a year apart. The older generation of parents, mine included, wisely spaced children's births within two or more years apart for economic reasons or convenience, depending on the prevailing social circumstances. In any case, I would love to verify my actual age when the opportunity arises. Consequently, I was reluctant to celebrate my birthday until when I believed I had hit seventy, the start of the bonus stage in life per Psalm chapter 90 of the Old Testament.

I was compelled to guess the date and the month I was born in order to apply for a passport to travel to the United States in 1971 for further studies. Since the year of birth (1942) was not an issue, I quickly guessed December 27, 1942, as my date of birth. Numerous people have looked at me and boldly guessed that I am ten years younger than I claim to be. However, I am stuck with that date up to this minute, and categorically, it is official. I couldn't forgo the opportunity to travel, study, and reside in the greatest country in the world simply because my parents were illiterate and obviously denied the civil rights of recording the births of their children including scores of other poor kids in the neighboring villages.

I invite you to ponder the highlights of trials and tribulations that God helped me overcome during the early stages of my "lifelong journey."

Endurance and Survival

Prior to declaration of a state of emergency in Kenya in 1952 (see Civil War Devastation notes below), life in the villages was natural and relaxed. The communities were content with whatever nature had in place. Parents had no gifts of economic planning or finances to worry about; we simply endured hardships.

First, we survived because we were born to extraordinarily positive parents who

- had no access to hospitals, medical facilities, supplies, nurses, or doctors

- had no prenatal care (mothers ate and drank anything while they were pregnant)

- never visited clinics, had no pregnancy tests or evaluations, did not get tested for diabetes, BP, and the likes.

No childbearing mother knew when they got pregnant or when the baby would be born. *Mary and Joseph, in the Holy Bible, is a world example. She gave birth naturally in a cow shed. Mary never knew the due date because she never knew when she got pregnant and had no access to a gynecologist. Jesus, the holy baby, was wrapped in simple garments and placed in a manger. By God's grace, no complications occurred. In the book of Luke 2:40, we read that baby Jesus "grew and became strong, he was filled with wisdom and the grace of God was upon him."*

- As we grew, we were put to sleep on our tummies on hard dirt floors and on wooded dry beds in dark rooms without mattresses and/or beddings.

- There were no medicines, baby formulas, or milk bottles.

- There were no toys, bicycles, swingers, or balls of any kind.

- The nearest playground had one soccer ball with repair patches all over and was for adults only.

- We lived in round, windowless, grass-thatched huts with lizards, rats, flees, jiggers, occasional snake visits, and roaches as "close relatives."

- At night while we slept, these creatures journeyed over our bodies and feasted on debris of food stuck in our fingertips, cleaned up the cracks on our heels, and trimmed off the finger- and toenails. Mild rat bites on toes and fingers were normal manicure—oops. You did not need an appointment to be serviced. "This was a dedicated and committed workforce—always on time." Some workers even reported ahead of time and idled around. As soon as the fires went off, silence kicked in, and snoring started, the coast was clear for cleanup to start. Lice, jiggers, and fleas were undocumented illegal residents and had already built mansions in hairs, shirt collars, underarms, and along threaded garment streets and corners.

- There were neither vaccinations nor clinics of any kind.

Treatments for measles, irritations, coughs, fevers, etc., were conducted via use of common herbs. If a child or adult got critically ill to a point where natural herbs would not suffice, especially when they couldn't eat or drink, they were let go. If a child was infected with measles, parents made a paste of mud from moles' virgin soil and smeared it over the whole body to minimize itching and scratching.

Infancy and Childhood

During infancy and childhood:

- We rode on moms' or older kids' backs and dads' shoulders.

- When the ride got tired, the rider walked assisted by a guiding hand.

- In those days, there were no cars/pickups/vans, motorcycles, roller skits, or wheelbarrows in my village.

- Later on, riding on the top of an open truck/land rovers or a pickup was always heavens for kids.

- We drank water from swift rivers, wells, or still pot containers/ swamps. Our palms were substitutes for bowls or cups to scoop water from a running river.

- There were no soft drinks, tea, ice cream, candies, or the likes of today.

- Common drinks were sour milk, fermented cereal-based drinks such as millet, sorghum, finger millet, green corn, etc.

- If there was a cup or some other utensil, everyone drank from it, and no one got sick. Washing the utensil before or after use was unnecessary. Foot and mouth and contagious diseases came lately.

- We ate natural real solid foods; no cereals, bread, butter, jam, or deserts.

- The word *obesity* or *heavy* were uncommon, and everyone, including adults, had normal weight. Only animals had fat.

Persistence and Perseverance

- Unquestionably, we stayed healthy by keeping busy and actively productive. We hung outside either on assigned tasks or playing between shifts!

- The younger ones, four years and below, could play all day within the vicinity with mild supervision of older kids or adults.

- Five years or older would work all day and play in the evenings, so long as they had the chore jobs completed prior to sunset or even after dark.

- We would continue playing until dinner time and even after dinner on moonlight nights until bedtime.

- Dinners were never on time because mothers worked all day until sunset, which was around 6:30 in the evening.

Anytime at all was good enough.

- Having dinner depended on the weather situations and the time that mothers returned home from their hefty tasks.

- Parents or guardians knew where the children were at all times.

- Grandparents, older siblings, and neighbors pitched in as necessary on a voluntary basis.

- There were no "paid" babysitting work assignments; a treat to a bite or a drink to the helper was all that mattered.

- With or without lunch, assignments were given daily in the morning, and no one questioned, argued, or underperformed.

- If a parent had to leave early in the morning, the instructions were communicated the previous night so mental processing and recordings were common among older kids.

- Disobedience and bad behavior were punished instantly. The parents solely determined the type, extent, and gravity of punishments.

- Mothers disciplined the girls while the fathers dealt with the boys.

- Some punishments could be executed by either parent depending on the seriousness of the violation. Often, the mother would initiate round one, and the father would wrap it up.

- Boys were assigned external chores that included herding, digging, fencing, wood splitting, and delivery of messages to close-by relatives/friends.

- Girls were involved in tasks such as babysitting younger siblings, washing, fetching water (there was no piped water system), collecting firewood, and cooking select dishes. Boiling hard dried cereals like corn and beans was routine. There were no complaints, grumbling, or squabbles.

- While herding, boys would spend hours building wooden hula hoops (*Thigo*) out of soft wild shrubs especially on days when goats were feeding in thick bushes.

- We swung on tree branches, on slopes, and mudslide using peeled banana stems (*Gutindaara na Mitindi*).

- We got injured frequently but did not inform the parents.

Careless injuries were greeted with additional beatings including denial of dinner on a particular night.

- Child abuse was never a part of the vocabulary or culture. A child could be disciplined by any adult in the village for bad behavior.

- Real bad kids were disciplined by a community council of tough adults—carefully selected by parents.

- There was no electricity, but there was enough firewood for cooking and warm-ups.

- There were no radios, videos, or Nintendos.

- Unlike modern times, there were no video games, TVs, movies, DVDs, or CDs.

- In addition, there were no personal computers, Internet, or Facebook.

- We got a new set of clothing only when the former sets were completely torn such that no further stitching or repairs would improve it. In other words, nothing went to waste, and nothing was left to give away. The retired sets were used as cleanup rags or dusters.

Friends and Playmates

Parents of our time did not select or recommend who should be your playmates. The relationships sort of came naturally. Boys interacted with boys and girls likewise. We were careful not to hurt each other. Instead, we looked out for each other gently and compassionately.

Visits to a neighbor's house were commonly impromptu and un-announced. On dangerous episodes we fell off trees, trenches, rocks, cliffs, got cut, nose bleeds, bruises from stumbles, broke limbs and teeth—you name it.

- There were no family health insurances or any type of health coverage.

- We ate wild fruits, roots, nuts, insects, worms, trapped birds and chicks, wild animal meat, and no stomach upsets. Remember the Israelis in the wilderness during the exodus from Egypt to the "Promised Land," Canaan? They ate manna daily for forty years, and nobody got sick. Prior to the fifties, domestic chicken were rare, and only roosters were slaughtered on occasions for special family guests.

The hens were preserved for laying eggs.

- Kites and hawks feasted on the chicks when they hatched and wandered out, and only a few out of a brood of roughly ten made it to adulthood.

- There were no bicycles—simply walked to a friend's house and called out the name of your friend or their mom.

Never asked for their dad. There were no doorbells, and upon welcome, you just walked in and greeted, talked, and socialized.

- Footpaths connected houses and villages and were communally maintained and remained clear of tree branches to allow safe passage and avoid injuries. We were verbally warned that tree branches and tall grass occasionally were habitats for poisonous snakes and spiders that could be harmful.

- The only community law was parental or community based. The idea of a parental pardon for a child when they broke the law was unheard of. All rules were enforced without exception.

- Any senior member of the community (parent, uncle, grandparent, and seniors) had the mandate to discipline any child who misbehaved. They had absolute autonomy to enforce the law at will! • There were no known thieves, and homes had no locking doors or security systems.

- Nothing got lost around the house because somebody knew the whereabouts of everything. So if something was missing or got messed up, somebody took responsibility.

Only misplacements were punished by reprimands. If no one took responsibility, then it became everybody's business, and all accountable parties paid the price.

- Based on these solid foundations, the earlier generations have produced some of the best risk-takers, daredevils, mentors, problem solvers, and even inventors.

- The past fifty years have been an explosion of innovative character building, self-reliance, critical thinking, ventures, and new high-tech ideas.

- We had freedom, challenges, failures, successes and responsibilities, love and compassion. We cared, shared, and exalted one another.

- And we learned how to deal with it all—forgive and forget.

If *you* are one of them generations, *well done*! "Those were the days."

- I almost forgot to mention that we obtained God-given immunity and bypassed the pass-through catastrophes spread by the viruses that were common in those days:

  - Pneumonia, itching, chicken pox, mops, meningitis, and the like.

  - Parasites such as jiggers, fleas, bedbugs, lice, mosquitos, etc., were vicious. Stings by bees, spiders, ticks, and other strangers also claimed their share. I for one got attacked by all of the above and was infested by each of the viruses except meningitis. No control disinfectants were available in the markets, just as there were no vaccinations to immunize the children or the adults. Parents used herbal medicines, but besides God, they had no one to turn to. The modern Ministries of Health

Services and "disease control centers" did not exist in those years.

Our parents were tough, courageous, full of faith, and lucky that we survived the cruel and ruthless times and lived to tell the stories. Who says there is no God? Well, if you do, you are wrong!

Birthdays and Holidays

- Nobody in my village, adult or child, ever celebrated their birthdays. We never had birthday celebrations, and the majority of kids did not know or care about their birthdays.

You are alive—that's what mattered.

- Kids under ten years of age celebrated birthdays of newly born kids a month after they were born to welcome them to a new world, and that was it. Such events were frequent since there were no birth control mechanisms of today.

Almost every childbearing mom had a baby every two to three years, so there was no basis for worrying about personal matters like birthdays. You were born, alive and well—so what's the big deal about a piece of cake?

- The mother of the infant would provide roasted corn, yams, bananas, cassava, sweet potatoes, and a choice of fermented gruel (*ucuru*). Kids would kindle a fire which included the cut hair (baby hair) of the newly born and dry grass from the roof of the mother's hut. The elements of the feast would be smoked on this fire and then consumed.

- The participating kids would sing selected folk songs, devour the elements, and, finally, stamp out the fire with bare feet.

Since the majority of kids were delivered at home, birthdays were rarely recorded because birth registrations were not required, and most people were illiterate. Some remembered the year they were born but not the specific dates. It was easy to remember the day of the week but rarely the date of the month. On the same token, no holidays were celebrated prior to Kenya's independence on December 12, 1963. Christmas was simply a religious season. Children aged over eight years formed groups and sang Christmas carols a week before Christmas from dark to whatever time they decided to stop.

The process involved moving from home to home. Those visited at homes would reward kids with food items, cooked or raw. Money and silver were uncommon. Until early fifties when cash crop (coffee, sisal, animal hides, and charcoal) was introduced in the economy, money was scarce, and the community used the barter system as medium of exchange. Thus, on Christmas day, families, including children groups, cooked special meals and visited friends and relatives.

I always volunteered as a chef for my group, a trait I have enjoyed and exploited to date. Under those circumstances, no tangible gifts were exchanged.

Today is a different story altogether. Kenya celebrates "Valentine's Day" among others.

All in all, moral character building was essential. A hearty character was an indelible and a valued community characteristic.

Folks felt that "Bad manners are worse than poverty." Ironically, bad manners are produced by poor character. Poverty, however, has no roots and can be economically eradicated. Over the years, experience and observations have convinced me that the basics for determining whether an act is good or bad are good common sense. In essence, common sense is a humanistic free gift from God! It is a terminal degree for both the literate and the illiterate communities at large.

Also, let me add that I am totally convinced that the "good spirit" is a free gift of God to mankind and, indeed, "The Almighty God created all men equal!"

Borrowing and Lending

The community norm permitted borrowing and lending of all sorts.

The following were among common transactions:

- Food items such as cooking oil, sugar, dishes, gardening tools, etc.

- Commodity exchange—goods for goods, livestock for livestock, and communal labor.

- Moneylending was rare due to scarcity, so just a few family units had access to the market.

- Children borrowed and exchanged clothing with age-mates or close relatives.

- Older folks borrowed able children to assist them with their daily chores at no cost except for provision of meals.

- Community events entailed all able bodies to come out and lend a hand freely.

Do We Need God's Favor?

Do we need God's immunity here on earth? With earthquakes, hurricanes, tornados, storms, typhoons, El Niño, global warming, wildfires, locusts, hunger, drought, whooping cough, kwashiorkor, natural calamities, mudslides, sinkholes, flash floods, hardcore criminals, radicalism, lawlessness, neighborhoods and city gangs, snapshooters, serial killers, internal and external conflicts, con artists, false prophets, cult advocates, fraud, corruption, wickedness, unscrupulous leaderships, cybercrime, sexual freedom, atheistic advocates—and you name it—these ideologies are tearing up the world from one continent to another, and with the threat of coronavirus, swine flu, Ebola, cancer, blood pressure, arthritis, HIV, venereal diseases, terrorist attacks, and, most recently, the coronavirus disease pandemic or COVID-19 for short.

My question is, are we sure that we are spiritually correct and that this is a good timing to take God out of our lives? The answer, of course, depends on what you believe. Personally, I believe it's worth noting that God has opened heavens as our final solace or retreat domain—safe haven.

Confession of faith in His son Jesus Christ who is the way, the truth, and the life will earn us "a change of status." Simply admit, apologize, and ask for a favor. It's your life—it's up to you to decide who you'll let go out of your life, who you'll let stay in your life, and who you'll trust with your life.

- When there is nowhere else to go, and one is stuck on a dead-end road or cave, that is when we realize we need God as a last resort for rescue.

- God has responded and placed the conditions for rescue in His holy Word—the "bible" (Best Instructions Before Leaving Earth). The passport and the visa lines to enter God's kingdom are empty. Quick advice—jump on line and obtain your travel documents, that is, the Passport and a Visa to heaven! Christ is the connecting bridge of hope between the two spheres.

- Note: The cost is absolutely free. All you need is confession of faith in Jesus Christ! God the father would provide mercy, grace, and seal it with the "Holy Spirit".

Personal Spiritual Life

It has been a lifetime struggle with spiritual life in a world dominated by the devil (the father of sin, deceit, and death) and contaminated with evil and darkness. However, by the power of God's gift of the Holy Spirit within me, the Bible reminds me that I can do all things through Christ.

I believe the willpower to write this life story was enabled by the work of the Holy Spirit of God and stimulated by my walk of faith in Christ since childhood (age twelve). Also, the thought was appetized by service as a former deacon and as a ruling elder (RE) in an Evangelical PCA church in America within the state of Maryland, USA, for over thirty-five years and attuned by service as chaplain, secretary, and treasurer with Gideon International Ministry in the Washington metropolitan for over twenty years while walking with God and away from home (motherland—Kenya) for fifty years. Now at age seventy-seven and going, I've maintained sanity; sound mind, body, and soul because of my daily walk with Christ, my Lord and defender. Also, I believe in the Apostles Creed.

Flashback

Kenya had officially become a colony in 1920, and Nairobi was the command center. For purposes of spreading the Colonial rule, ideology, and influence, the empire had initiated and encouraged church-planting missionary work, hospitals, schools including largescale farming of one-mile squires (640 acre tracks) in the fertile Kenyan Rift Valley region. Earlier on, the colonists had mapped out administrative centers around Kenya and were strategically established in the west, east, north, south, and the central regions within the colony. Accordingly, denominations such as Anglican, Catholic, Methodist, Protestants, etc., came into existence. These were indeed the real colonizers but were in the guise of "shepherds dressed in sheepskins." The Islam had already mushroomed and spread along the coastal lines, trading centers, and townships during the slave trade era. The Islam faith just filled the blanks.

A case in point: Chogoria Hospital, Mission, and School in Meru County today served as a birthplace for the Presbyterian Church of East Africa (PCEA) effective 1922. Smaller community churches and denominational schools also unfolded. The community churches were led by local elders, and the area schools up to fourth grade were taught by eighth graders. Kiangua, Rachi's home village, is just five miles from Chogoria, but the stated institutions became functional in the midforties. Tug of war and resentments between the rebel church groups were intense. The recruitment of the locals into joining the competing sects through offers of free education and other goodies did not succeed. The promoters offered these incentives secretly without public announcements. Probably the corruption elements of nepotism might have hatched during that time. Consequently, religious advancements stalled remarkably, and social events were apparently chaotic. Also in the mix were the traditional and independent community organizations that did not support any ideologies or advocacy relative to change in ancestral and cultural norms (circumcisions, marriages, folk dances, rites, and events).

Notwithstanding the aforementioned negative forces at the time, Rachi accepted Christ in a broad-day-light first PCEA open-air crusade in my village. The words that echoed over the loudspeaker were, "Come unto me all of you that are heavy laden and I will give you rest." Later, I learned that the gorgeous words that took my breath away were taken from the New Testament book of Matthew 11:28. I came to Jesus, found peace and rest, and I was "home at last"!

Today, as I continue my "faith journey," I am convinced that I highly cherish the biblical encouragement recorded in the book of Ephesians 2:19–20, among others, that, "We are no longer foreigners and aliens. Instead we are fellow citizens with God's people and members of God's household, built on the foundation of the saints and prophets, with Jesus himself as the Chief cornerstone."

Thank God that believers are no strangers or foreigners to the Word of God. We have been accepted into God's family, and we have been classified as His children, even stretching further that we are "born of God." This is an incredible identity—that we are coheirs with Christ. So be it. The fact that we are safe in our Father's arms all the days of our lives and beyond is second to none. My personal gratification is that I inherit three citizenships (i.e., A Kenyan, an American by choice, and biblically promised "fellow citizen" of God's kingdom). What a joy of relief and comfort!

Personally, I recognize the Bible as holy, inspired, inerrant, infinite, and that it contains the mind of God, the state of man, the way of salvation, the doom of sinners, and the happiness of believers.

Its doctrines are holy, its precepts are binding, its histories are true, and its decisions are immutable. I read it to be wise, believe it to be safe, and practice it to be righteous. It contains light to direct a believer, food for the soul, comfort and hope for rejoicing. Simply, "Jesus is the way, the truth, the life, and Lord of all."

Note: It is proper to read the Word of God over and over in order to gain the understanding of eternal truth that if anyone searches the Word of God for light, with a heart fully committed to do the will of God as it is revealed to him/her by the "Holy Spirit," that person will receive the light. In John 14:6 Jesus said, "I am the way, the truth and the life. No one comes to the Father except through me." That's it—case closed. The skin color of Jesus is irrelevant. "God is a spirit!"

Observation: God's salvation for mankind is made simple in John 3:16: Jesus Christ is our Lord and Savior. We have been called o simply believe that He came to earth as a man, died on the cross for our sins, and resurrected on the third day. There are no other requirements to receive salvation—God made it that simple for mankind.

This is what believers need to let the world know so that they can tell it on the mountains, valleys, villages, supermarkets, and towns that Jesus Christ is Lord! That all can partake of God's great love and free inheritance of His riches.

Now, a retired professor, I taught auditing, cost accounting, managerial accounting, and advanced accounting courses, business management, finance, and economics at the schools of business within Washington metropolitan area (University of DC, University of Maryland, and Southeastern University); a scholar, professional accountant, auditor, programs analyst/inspector, counselor, consultant, entrepreneur, writer, parent, grandfather, community leader, and family patriarch.

I had the opportunity to serve the US Federal Government as an accountant, analyst, auditor and programs inspector in the Office of Inspector General within the Department of Justice under "Top Secret Security Clearance" ranking for many years. Prior to migrating to the United States in 1971, I had served the Republic of Kenya as an administrative assistant and cost accountant for the East African Railways and Harbours for eleven years.

Moreover, I received numerous academic achievement awards, diplomas, scholarships, monetary awards, performance certificates, and numerous honorariums.

God's providence: By God's grace, I am who I am, where I am, what I am, have what I have, and no desire for what God doesn't want me to have; and so, to God be the glory!

Appetite for Education: Primary Schooling

I was the first one in my family and my village to pioneer into the academic education. The first elementary school opened in my village in 1946. I was only four years old at that time. My parents and other local residents had not been exposed to any formal schooling, so to them, the concept of schooling was strange and meaningless.

In 1949 at the age 7, I had noticed kids my age from other villages dressed better and talking languages I did not understand. They would talk about mathematics: adding, subtraction, division, and multiplication. They talked about spelling of vernacular words (local dialect), actually reciting what they had learned at school that day. This happened mostly in the afternoons. I noticed that first and second graders had classes for half a day. That allowed them to stay home after lunch. Third and fourth graders returned to school after lunch and studied up to 4:00 p.m. Sporting activities were held up to 6:00 p.m. Kids travelled a radius of four miles one way to school.

The chant inspired me, and I personally decided to take a calculated risk and give it a shot. One weekday without informing anyone, I camped on the outskirts of the school compound late in the morning. My father had already delegated and entrusted me with the responsibility of shepherding or looking after a herd of thirty goats.

Typically, all I did was take the animals out of the homestead, select a shrubby ground with plenty of edible leaves or grass, and let them browse freely. Goats are hyper and move frequently and require constant control, confinement, and direction. My father had frequently oriented me regarding these skills and warned me that I would beheld responsible and accountable for failure to ensure enforcement.

Goats could be devastating to young plantations and crops such as maize or beans. If allowed they would devour plants and crops to ground zero. The occasion is akin to salad or an appetizer to a human meal time.

Influenced by my appetite for school, I imagined that my animals would behave themselves and continue feeding on a very suitable area that I had carefully selected. You see, I had noticed that the classrooms at school had no windows. That way, I could standup and visualize the whereabouts of the goats if at all they moved.

With the plan in place, I left the animals unattended, entered the school compound, walked up to a classroom, and entered the nearest classroom from my point of entry. The notion of how the classrooms were arranged did not matter to me.

Immediately, a male teacher noticed me approaching and came forward to meet me. He asked me what I needed, and I answered that I had come to start school. He asked whether this was my first time at school, and I said yes. At that point, he decided I was a beginner and remarked that I belonged to sub-A or first grade and volunteered to escort me to this new location. I had no clue what that meant, but I followed him anyway. As we walked, I noticed that eyes were peeping through the bare windows gazing at me, and

I started getting nervous. My escort met someone along the path, probably another teacher, and handed me over to this stranger. My escort instructed the stranger to take me to *kandurumo*. Later on, I learned this word meant "first grade." To me, however, it meant a "waterfall," a swift river where people drowned. I immediately reacted with a loud "No…no!" I screamed and begged not to be taken there, a desperate cry of a beginner scholar. When the stranger hesitated, I took off crying and running as fast as I could. I could hear sounds of laughter behind me, but when I turned and looked, no one was pursuing me.

As I made all these moves, I was fully determined to be a pupil. The sudden turn of events almost ruined my academic goal and vision.

The thought of counting, spelling, and reading like those children who passed through my neighborhood daily was all that jammed my thoughts.

I instantly suspended the schooling initiative for that day and tried to get myself together and refresh. Mind you, I was still terrified, and my heart was racing and beating hard. Meanwhile, the thought of the animals soon came back. The goats and I regrouped. Fortunately, despite the goats having wandered away to some adjacent areas, no damage occurred; but clearly, that was a narrow escape. I moved the animals away from the school area on that day and did not wish to come into contact with anyone at school. As you can envision, I met two-thirds of the whole school within minutes. I might have looked funny. You see, I had not taken a bath or changed clothes for who knows when. All I remember is that I had one, and only one, old cut-size piece of "Chuka," the equivalent of half a sheet of a twin bed. Washing required wetting the garment in a spring water or river or use some special leaves that produced some soap like foam (*Matuntu* and *Mathiru-thiru*); for example, squeeze as much dirt out of the garment as you could then rinse and let dry, spread out in the sun. The hotter the sun the better because you stayed naked and needed the garment back on soonest. You preferred complete solitude at a time like this—no company, no public exposure, period.

I never regained enough courage to reenter school until a year later. There were lots of school-related details that I was not aware of such as:

1. School started in a particular month

2. Uniform—not required but whatever you had on must be clean

3. Tuition—was mandatory (KSh 2 or 25 American cents)

4. Parental permission—required

5. Age was not an issue—admission policy was "Any child, any age, any dress code . . . just as you are" to attract new entrants.

When I sought my dad's permission, he denied pronto. My father stressed that his number one priority was that I continue to shepherd the animals, period. We didn't even touch on the tuition issue because I did not understand anything about money. So, I was doomed momentarily since my academic dream had been crushed.

Out of desperation and the desire to get started, I recalled that one of my uncles on my father's side "Kcira Mwenda" had relocated to another neighborhood due to grazing problems. He owned cows and sheep and needed a sizable grazing area. About three valleys away from our village, a friend had allowed him to relocate and occupy the friend's land. My uncle had a son about my age. His name was Samuel. So I visited them to see how they were doing. I was impressed with the environment especially the size and quality of the animal food. Without hesitation, I shared my pending academic plan with my uncle by explaining that I will move the goats over to the area; my cousin Samuel would watch over them. In the morning while I attended school (half a day); I'll pass by our home and bring food for dinner; and I'll take over watching the flock for the rest of the afternoon.

This sounded fabulous to the pair. What a relief, I thought.

The stage was set. By January 1949, I was among the top ten to vie for a position in first grade. By God's grace, I got admitted, but there was a crippling dilemma—I had no money for tuition. During the make-it-work time, we had kept my father out of the loop. My mum, however, had concurred and was okay with "plan B" but had cautioned me not to give my father any clue that she was part of it.

My father would feel betrayed if such cover ups come to light. Well, realizing my predicament, the area school principal became sympathetic.

He was the school's first principal; therefore, he had witnessed several identical cases in the past. He remembered my image from the previous encounter a year earlier (crying and running). He asked whose son I was, and when I mentioned my father's name, he remarked that we had a problem. Big problem! He knew my father well. He was tough, violent, conservative, and a diehard.

Nonetheless, the principal agreed to accompany me the next day for a nasty confrontation with my father. At first sight of the teacher, my father frowned, paused, and asked the teacher, "Why is my son with you, and what are you doing here?"

The teacher answered, "Your son has to start schooling, and he needs twenty-five cents school fees from you."

My father replied he had no money (true) and that if he allowed me to abandon the herd and instead attend school, I am not his son, and the teacher could have me as his son if he wished. My father asked me directly if that was my sole intent, and I said yes! At that point, my father ordered that both of us leave the compound or deal with the aftermath.

The teacher knew the answer better, and he and I departed pronto. On the way back to school, the teacher agreed to sponsor me by paying the initial school fee until my father calmed down, provided I was ready to take the challenge. I answered in the affirmative.

The next day I was at school. By this time, I knew what *kandurumo* meant—a dark classroom in a corner of the school building without a door, had hollow windows, no lights, and no desks. The kids sat on flat wood offcuts nailed to round wooden pegs on unpaved dusty floors. No one had shoes on. I did not have any such luxury at home, so no problem.

School and I became the best of friends. All subjects and topics were fun, fun, fun including playing with other boys during short breaks. I likened school to finding hidden treasure within reach.

While in third grade, the teacher had his students close the day's activities with the following motivational song:

"Today's battles are fought by educational tools..."

Inform the inquirer that

- a pencil is the spear,

- the book is the shield, and

- the soldiers are the students and the commanders are the teachers.

The same teacher reminded us to be back the next day for more knowledge in readiness for future "academic wars."

The only mode of transportation to and from school was walking and running. To a kid like me, this was a welcome daily hobby, and both the goats and my dad were no longer a stumbling block.

Peter, my principal friend, monitored my progress closely. Based on my academic achievement for the first six months, the school decided to upgrade and moved me to second grade. In second grade, I continued to perform even better than those that were in class from the beginning of the year and probably some of those that laughed and jeered at me a year earlier when I ran for my life after getting scared of *kandurumo*. By God's grace, the twenty-five-cent school fees that got me started took care of the two classes since it was within the same year. Huge thanks to my teacher-friend, Peter. Nice, eh?

Subsequently, I moved to third grade and progressed well. By late 1950, my dad planted one hundred coffee trees. This was a cash crop, but it took a minimum of three years before cashing in on it.

Therefore, the first payout was realized during 1953. In 1951, my father had accepted a construction job and had relocated to Nairobi.

Consequently, my mother had already planned for me to return home with the animals that I had adjoined earlier with uncle Kuira and had my younger brother take over the herding task. Uncle Kuira had raised a mild concern that my inability to assist with the herds in the afternoons, as previously agreed, had created a burden to both him and my cousin. Actually, my attending third grade all day curtailed my prior year participation substantially, you see. The joint plan with my mother had considered the fact that my brother was not tough and brave enough to take on the assignment away from home. He was not keen on details and lacked patience. However, he had taken quite a number of lessons and practical exposures, so we reasoned that he'd grow and grasp these traits during daily exercise.

Just remember that third and fourth graders schooled all day, and that impaired my animal-herd project. Instead, I assisted Mom on weekends with gardening and other chore duties since my father was away.

Honestly, I do not recall how I fared on with school fees. The fact that I was still at school was obvious that my mom might have somehow worked a viable plan. I did not dare to ask. I simply trusted that God was in control and providing. Oh yes!

Early in 1951, I convinced my older sister Eunice to attempt school. By nature, she was rather shy. We realized during her early childhood that she had limited body immunity and often fell sick.

With no hospitals to go to, she did not heal well. Upon my persistence and, of course, with my mom's permission and encouragement, she agreed. I warned her though that she'd be alone in her class, and that made her very nervous. I assured her she would be all right and advised her to just be calm despite what anybody might say to her. Less than an hour after classes started, I realized some commotion, jeers, and laughs in the direction of her *kandurumo* class (first grade). Guess what? My sister was on the run homeward. I figured what had happened even without questions. She completely forgot about me. At home during lunch break my sister shared that she felt so intimidated by some kids who were total strangers to her. She explained that some called her bad names. Whatever the names were, she resented school, developed phobia, and no longer stepped into a classroom in subsequent years. However, she beat the odds, grew up tough, and got circumcised in the village in 1952. Her ailments diminished, and she became fairly healthy and knowledgeable. She later got married, had children, and was a grandmother at the time she passed on to glory at age 74. The Lord blessed her soul.

Sometime later in 1951 while in third grade, my father surprised me by gifting me with my first ever pair of short-sleeve shirt and shorts. Obviously, his construction job at Nairobi had started bearing fruit. I looked like you never saw. Incidentally, I was the first kid in the entire village to own such an outfit, and I was so humbled.

Also, I attracted a lot of attention at school. I imagined I will never again dress any lesser, and the dream became a reality as I continued to overcome academic challenges. Thanks be to God.

Even without shoes or underwear at the time, I felt like somebody's son and gave my father a silent salute. In 1952, I sat for my first national examination popularly known as the "Common Entrance Examination" (CEE). Ten out of a class of thirty-five students passed.

I was one of the ten.

In 1953, five of the ten joined a boarding school, and five joined a day school then known as "Primary Tops" for fifth graders.

My primary top was exactly five miles away from my village. The twenty-five that failed the exam either repeated or were sent home for good.

My four friends and I were on this roller coaster for a whole year, and I can boldly state that it was one of the roughest academic tours for the group. Right on the outset we were informed that the school did not have breakfast, lunch, or snack programs. That meant that everybody took a compulsory lunch break, and, sadly, any form of eating was not allowed on school premises. Alternatively, the long-distance students (two or more miles) brought food items and hid them in the surrounding bushes or trees. There was a problem with that though. The unschooling local boys and area students would come out early, spy on the incoming out-of-area students, spot and mark the locations of the hidden treasure, sneak out during breaks before lunch time, and retrieve, eat, or hide the treasure somewhere else or just dash out fast when the lunch bell rang, take our lunch, and run off home with it. After the first two weeks of school, the burglary became unbearable.

We abandoned the effort, brought nothing from home, and starved throughout the day. Occasionally when we had money change, we would visit a local market and snack on sweet bananas or beat the bushes in search of wild berries, fruits, roots, etc. The sporting evenings at school (Monday, Wednesday and Friday) were the toughest because the events started at 4:15 p.m. and ended at 5:45 p.m. In the morning we came in running, often without breakfast, and had to go home running on an empty stomach. It was difficult making friends around the school because of the way we were initially received, intimidated, treated, and the fact that the teachers did not demonstrate humane concerns or care for our welfare. We later learned from the sixth graders from our locality that the folks in the surrounding areas had an ongoing general dislike or call it a "grudge"

against us (students from other jurisdictions). Since our counterpart students had outgrown the animosity, they advised us not to mind the tensions. To date, I have never endeavored to dig out the root cause. Anyhow, whatever the cause was, we felt the effect—our spirits were broken to pieces. Some of the older boys were bullies, but we intentionally avoided any form of direct confrontation to limit hostility.

My fellow classmate and I secretly carried slings and carefully selected rocks and hid these in our book bags just in case. God forbade, no occasion arose for use of these gadgets. That was a real close call!

Despite trials and tribulations, we persevered throughout the 1953 school year.

Just to add insults to an injury, the headmaster dropped a bomb by coldly announcing during end-of-year closing festivities that the Colonial government had determined to discontinue and close all the primary top school programs (fifth and sixth grades) countrywide effective December 31, 1953. He simulated that these classes would be replaced by new intermediate school schemes—fifth through eighth grades—effective January 1954. Without any remorse or hesitation, we were advised to seek admission on our own to any open intermediate school and were given a listing of existing schools in our region. That was it! To most of us, this was the equivalent of a "sudden death" just like in sports. The 90 percent of the affected students were pioneers in their families and had no idea of what to think or do, leave alone who to consult. The majority of the academic dreams for those in fifth and sixth grades were shattered once and for all. I counted up to 60 percent—me included—that became instant victims. Now, with the academic dream destroyed and roads closed, I returned home emotionally disturbed and heartbroken.

I tried to explain the case to my mom, but it did not go that well either. She had the notion that I probably did something messy that resulted into expulsion from school. I protested by advising her to visit any of the families of my colleagues who knew the facts as well as I did and could elaborate the story. Well, she did agree and took the steps. She returned remarkably torn apart and dismayed.

We cried together, prayed, and resolved to regroup later for envisioning.

My father was still away in his construction job in Nairobi. Meanwhile, another dark crowd came into the vicinity. Little did we know that the worst family catastrophe was right on the doorsteps. The civil war, or the "Mau Mau" uprising, had infested the Central Province of Kenya of which Meru District was part of. Now at home, twelve years old, with no school assignments, I inherited most of the household tasks, the likes of harvesting coffee; mulching; weeding in the banana, yams, sugar canes, and other plantations.

The family owned six acres of farmland that was fully developed, and labor was necessary. We could not afford hired labor, so what you see is what you get. Mom and I were well coordinated and made a swell team. She recognized my leadership potential, trusted my skills, and delegated chunks of her authority to me.

The Catastrophes of the Mau Mau Uprising

Overview

Earlier on in the flashback section of this book, I highlighted that the colonial rule was officially imposed upon Kenya and made it a British colony in 1920. Nairobi became the administrative command center.

After thirty years of suppression and discriminatory era, the Mau Mau uprising began in 1952 as **an opposition to these inequalities and injustices within the colony**. To counter act, the British announced a state of emergency in Central Province of Kenya during this same year. The response of the colonial administration was a fierce crackdown on the rebels, resulting in deaths of tens of white-settlers and hundreds of British police and army soldiers. The Kenyan freedom fighters, civilians and other victims perished in thousands.

Key issues such as expulsion of Kikuyu tenants from white-settler farms, loss of land to settlers, poverty, and, lack of true political representation for Africans contributed the steam for the revolt. Consequently, there was a huge increase in the number of Kikuyus migrating to urban cities; leading to economic chaos, unemployment and, overpopulation.

The reason that the revolt was majorly limited to the Kikuyu people was, in part, that they had suffered the **most as a result of the negative aspects of British colonialism**. The neighboring people of Embu and Meru joined the movement simply as sympathizers and on a comradery basis. In fact, there were no real white settlements in Embu and Meru except in areas around missionary centers. The missionaries had grabbed sizeable pieces of adjusting prime land under the guise that they will build and maintain free schools, health clinics, and hospitals. When the promised infrastructures became operational, the administrators demanded money for services despite their awareness that the majority of the local populations could not afford such fees for lack of reliable sources of income. This state of affairs angered the locals and created mutual tensions and resentments.

Essentially, the Mau Mau Rebellion was a militant African nationalist movement active in Kenya during the 1950s. Its primary goal was **"overthrowing British rule and removing European settlers from the country."**

In essence, the British reacted by: **creating detention camps** for Central Province suspects and elements of sympathizers suspected of being associated with the Mau Mau, including the elderly and children. Methodologically, the crown exercised extreme torture to gather information and to limit uprisings. According to archived information, over one million central Kenya residents were forcibly removed from their homes and put into isolated detention camps. Painfully, the process **entailed massive round-ups of suspected Mau Mau and supporters, with large numbers of suspects hanged, castrated, or tortured to death, and hundreds of thousands held in detention camps for long periods (1-7) years**

with no compensation, visitation, or human rights. Many Mau Mau rebels and armies established their bases in the Mt. Kenya Forest, the mountains of Aberdares, and secret caves and escarpments within Embu and Meru.

End result: By 1957 through 1960, the Mau Mau terrorist armies were remarkably broken. Abruptly, the British government declared the emergency over. Simultaneously, the British government implemented the initially sought political and economic reforms. Three years later, in 1963, Kenya received its independence from Great Britain and Jomo Kenyatta, the alleged master minder and top leader of the clandestine Mau Mau movement, became the first president of the new Republic of Kenya. He was elected unopposed under the Kenya African National Union (KANU) ticket. Kenyatta had served a 7-year detention term and had been released in 1961. He reigned until 1978 when he succumbed to a natural death while still in office.

As mentioned above, my father lived in Nairobi, where he worked for the contractor that built the Kenyan High Court buildings in the Kenyan Capitol. While still at work in Nairobi during 1952, the Mau Mau civil uprising emerged. I was in class 4 then, getting ready for the finals and the national exams then commonly known as the Common Entrance Exam (CEE). Later on, we learned that my father had secretly joined the movement by taking two oaths of allegiance to demonstrate the support for the movement. However, in late 1953, he developed chest pains and congestion attributed to the work environment (inhaling dust and polluted air) at work. He got admitted at the King George's Hospital, the then national hospital which was later renamed Kenyatta Hospital after independence. By the time he got discharged from the hospital, a state of emergency had been declared in Central Province, Nairobi, and some specific surroundings in Kenya because of the Mau Mau uprising. The state of affairs was real tense in Nairobi. Consequently, my father was given a choice of a one-way ticket by public transportation to Meru town or stay in Nairobi where he could be arrested any time should he have participated in oathtaking. Of course, knowing that he had taken the oath, he foresaw the risk and resolved to abandon all his belongings in Nairobi and return home directly while it was still safe.

He made it home safely. With only a few months' rest at home, my father was picked up for screening. That was it—he was instantly detained without trial and never returned home. Sadly, no one saw my father anymore except son Rachi, the writer of this story, until 1958 when he returned home after serving a six-year detention sentence for *being a member of an outlawed movement so-called* MAU MAU. When he did not return home within a few days following the arrest, my mother dispatched me to "Igoji" detention camp where area Mau Mau suspects were temporarily detained for initial screening.

I took with me some homecooked food and a sour drink (*ucuru*). Sure enough, that is where he was with his body swollen up from head to toes. I started thinking that a swarm of bees had been poured onto his naked body. However, when we had a chance to talk despite impaired speech, he shared that he had obtained the injuries during an intense two-day interrogations and torture by the home guards (*Kaborio*) at the interrogatory center. In fact, he was unable to eat the food and only sipped the *"ucuru"* drink. He could not move his jaws. To save the treat, he invited his

55

prescreened cellmates to help themselves with the elements. They devoured every bit, and I simply took the empty utensils home with me. At home, except my Mom, nobody wanted to hear my report. What I told her shook her quite a bit. I attempted to go revisit him three days later only to learn that he had been moved to another camp that was not disclosed to me or the family. Evidently, he was prosecuted following admission that he had taken the Mau Mau oath. The way they tortured him left no option for holding off—guilty as charged even without representation!

From that time on, all I remember is praying continually that God will keep him safe and return him home someday.

After serving a full-term six-year detention, the Colonial government freed him without any form of compensation. He returned home with nothing but a withered body, poor health, loss of memory, impaired speech, withdrawn, and broke to the bone. Upon release, he was transported to his nearest town—Igoji, just the spot where his detention journey had commenced six years ago—and walked six miles to our home. The dilapidated hut that he had built ten years earlier became his dwelling quarters one more time. Upon return, and by God's grace, my father did not have a serious need for medical care. Luckily, he did not develop additional illnesses or side effects. He stayed healthy throughout. Personally, I thought he needed a physical checkup, but it did not matter to him that much.

He was blessed to be back home and alive. He narrated how he witnessed fellow detainees get castrated, maimed, clubbed to death, die of weird illnesses without treatment, got shot from behind when they attempted to escape, or just random massacres and exterminations.

Following dad's arrest, the roundup for Mau Mau activists and suspects continued from house to house, and everyone, including middle-age children, were considered suspects. I, for one, had taken the first round of oath secretly, and no one knew. No one talked about the Mau Mau movement openly. Oathtaking was a top secret, and little did I know that my mom and my older sister had taken the oath and were suspects. Surprise, surprise, surprise. Out of shock, my siblings, neighbors, and passersby witnessed my older sister and my mother being arrested and whisked away into detention as well. This happened barely two months after my father's arrest.

My Education Progress Disrupted

Ironically, without notice or preparation, I instantaneously assumed the role of "head of the household" and took charge of my four younger siblings, eighteen goats, four sheep, one hundred coffee trees, gardens, and plantations of *igwa*, *matuuma*, *nkwa*, *rukwaji*, and *rurigu* on the family land.

Eric, our baby brother, was just two and half years when our mom got snatched by the Colonial rulers. I did the best I could to feed him and bathed him once in a blue moon when soap became available, which was very rare. The older siblings, Geoffrey, Joyce, and Flora, simply washed their hands and splashed their faces. I knew we looked funny, but who cared?

The only source of income was coffee payout, but it was administratively blocked and unavailable for the farmers who had a family member in the forest or in detention for indulgence in Mau Mau freedom activities. Ngaine's family, as we now know, had three members in that category. To make the matter worse, I had no power of attorney to handle family finances. Nonetheless, with help from friends and sympathizers, we maintained, harvested, and delivered the coffee to the factory on a regular basis. I figured there would be quite a bit of money in the account when Mom finally got access to it. The other special blessing to the family was Kaaria's name. Despite having taken the Mau Mau oath, the name never resurfaced. The Almighty God shielded me while my enemies were blinded. I did not dare to imagine what could have happened to the family if anything had happened to me. I prayed and God heard my cries and He answered. Remarkably, God protected all of us including the older family members in detention, and thank God, no one got seriously sick or became a victim of other mishaps. The siblings and I bonded well except for Geoffrey and Joyce, who were hard cores off and on.

On occasions, I spanked Geoffrey for being careless and sloppy, but Flora and Eric were little darlings and were easy to direct. They probably thought I was their dad because of the way I cared for them. Uncle Mwamba on my mother's side was a home guard employed by the Colonial government at the time. He checked on us often and worked with me closely. I might mention here that the three uncles on Mom's side had taken the oath. First, uncle Ndegwa joined the movement and retreated into the forest as a freedom fighter in 1953 to avoid screening and detention. However, he perished in the struggle, and his remains were never recovered. He left behind a widow, and his five kids became fatherless. Only two of the youngest are still alive today. Second, uncle Nkaabu, just like my father, got arrested in Nairobi and was sentenced to a six-year detention term. He survived the ordeal but was in poor health due to torture and abuse while in detention. He finally passed on to glory in 2014 at 101. Uncle Mwamba survived the hard times, retired, but God called him home when his heart failed in 2012. He was ninety-four.

Meanwhile, during this rough time for the family, I had enticed my grandmother to come and live with us and assist me with housekeeping chores especially cooking. After some discussion and the fact that no one else needed her help at the time, she yielded. Uncle Mwamba and I had refurbished my dad's hut for her to settle in temporarily. Her voluntary contributions were immeasurable. However, even though grandmother helped as much as she could, my thoughts and feelings were heavy. The set of circumstances were real rough for me. For a twelve-year-old kid, this was a heck of a load on my back, and I never saw any end to it. Optionally, I prayed continually for any of the seniors to safely return home. God heard my prayers and allowed Mom to return home after almost a year since detention. Upon arrival at home, she broke into tears when she realized we were all alive despite our general health and physical appearances. Of course, we ate whatever food was available, wore overused and torn-up clothing. Until this time, none of us had set eyes on each other. We didn't know the whereabouts of her detention during the ordeal nor did she have a clue regarding our set of circumstances until this time. God just reunited us for His own glory and for our universal joy, at last. What a relief from daily worries and anxieties! Sister Eunice came home a year later following Mom's release.

About six months prior to her release, we learned that she was among the group that cleaned up the grounds and buildings at a Catholic diocese just six miles away from home, so we were able to visit her occasionally. I made most of the trips because Mom was now home, and, as noted earlier, I was out of school following the closure of my former middle school. Overall, my sister was detained for two years.

Village Circumcision to Manhood

Since Mom was now home and had alleviated some of my daily chores quite substantially, I had a sigh of relief including a window of opportunity to get the "initiation to manhood" project out of the way. Since my father was still away in detention, I asked my uncle on the mother's side for permission, and he concurred to step in as a substitute. Immediately during August, I jump-started the dialogue.

Since I had attained circumcision or the "cutting" age to manhood, both my mother and my uncle endorsed the plan. From there, it was just a matter of ranking the events in terms of priorities.

Traditionally, the "circumcision season" had always been during the month of December. Three months' prep lead time was considered sufficient. Accordingly, I proudly went through the traditional cutting ceremony along with eleven other boys in the village that lined up for the festivities.

By December 4, 1954, I officially became a junior warrior (*Ntaane*) within the Mwiro clan in the community. The boys went through every step as narrated in the following pages. In the naming ceremony a few months later, I was renamed Rachi, which I have used as my first name to date. Rachi is short for affable, the equivalent of an extrovert in the modern world character-wise. Naturally, I have a tendency to reach out and touch, care, and share. This characteristic is still alive in my heart, and I sense and feel it continually.

The Traditional Circumcision Norm

The customary cutting order required boys of older (senior) parents to be the first in line followed by those of younger parents—similar to "first come first served" pecking order in America. The order is supported by the notion that "a sharp knife has an easy cut and less pain." On the contrary, "a blunt knife is inefficient, cuts roughly, takes longer, and prolongs pain." I was ranked sixth on the lineup.

The process takes approximately five to ten minutes per client and starts at predawn (before sunrise) or early in the morning. No time clock, no numbing, no music, and no cheers, just warlike repetitive but rhythmic tribal choruses. The surgical team carried limited sets of knives just in case.

The cutting ceremony was preceded by a cold birth in a ceremonial river site within the community. The cold dip helped to numb the foreskin so it would ease the pain and limit blood flow. Rhythmic warlike songs and choruses of encouragement were sang and chanted loudly by active warriors throughout the ceremony. Phobia, breaking down, groaning, moaning, crying, or cowardly body movement during the cutting were outlawed and considered a taboo that could result in death upon the violator. The fresh initiates, or circumcisees, sat on wet grass naked, facing Mount Kenya to the North, with their heads turned sideways. The community believed that God lived on this mountain, and He would protect the fearful ones. Select young warriors initiated two to three years earlier assisted the initiates by kneeling behind them and supported their backs to allow firmness. Hands placed firmly on knees and biting firmly on the teeth and taking long systematic breaths in a relaxed manner was known to ease pain and detract attention from the ongoing live surgery. The circumciser leaned forward, bent his knees, and did his thing. The timing and speed depended upon the operator's experience and skills.

He simply played offence while the "circumcisee" played defense by playing bravely and courageously. Sweating, bleeding, and breathing were allowed. Penalties for expressed fear were brutal (mentioned earlier) and resulted into the victim being eliminated from the society by murder or given away freely to a remote community as an outcast. The culprit was considered a bad omen to his family, clan, and the underlying community, so killing or giving him away eliminated the awful memories.

Parents of the condemned party were completely in accord with this consensus.

In the warm-up stages (two months prior), the veteran warriors volunteered and shared heroic incidents and stories to the initiates in an effort to inspire courage. They coached, counseled, and sternly warned the "circumcisees"—locally known as *ndamari*—of the dire consequences associated with violations of established norms.

Instead, they should come out prepared to defend their manhood—live in dignity or perish. Notably, this was a super graduation from boyhood to junior warriorship (Ntaane). It was a show-off time and gratitude for respective families. It was a moment for self-gratification.

In America, the event could resemble the enactment of a retired star player onto the Hall of Fame in Canton, Ohio—very special.

The boys of age that might have lived outside the vicinity had to be rounded up randomly and escorted home by their relatives to join the ranks. If a boy of age had this ritual performed elsewhere, there had to be two credible eyewitnesses. The alternative option was to strip him naked privately and have him examined by select experts. i am! or i was! proclamation in the absence of these facts did not count.

Those caught cheating were stripped naked and cut in broad daylight with spectators watching. The revered penalty occurred rarely since the *ndamaris* were adequately prepared and had nothing to hide. Sometimes it took three to six months to get ready. Personally, I never learned of a recorded event of cowardice (jumping the knife).

In essence, when such incidents occurred, if any, they were handled in secrecy and confidentiality with no likelihood of leaks. Remember, a taboo resembled a curse, and avoiding occurrence was the best way out. Under normal circumstances, the healing of the cut wound would last four to six weeks. Actually, it would take longer if the cut became septic or became infected due to poor hygienic conditions.

No form of modern medication was allowed during the healing process. If that happened, the whole process would be deemed substandard and lose essence.

The community viewed such practices as norm violations—cheating, of course, and the "rookies" may not receive full recognition for due warrior status. Some boys, whose parents were/are less patriotic or pertain to modern religious sects, chose to get cut at the hospital. The procedures for this version of cleansing for manhood were/are less rigorous, modified, and tolerable. Based on hearsay, the foreskins get tranquilized prior to cutting. During my time, they were nicknamed *iroge* (plural) or *kiroge* (singular), implying that their manhood was medically boosted. Within two or three weeks, the *iroges* were home and free to roam about. However, the classification of their warrior status was technically considered moderate or substandard. However, that has changed over the years because the societal standards, especially health and religious beliefs, have drastically shifted toward moderate ideologies. Ideally, 95 percent of ageready boys are now circumcised in hospitals while the remaining 5 percent are homemade and secretive. Ironically, though, private but illegal cutting of females, popularly known as female genital mutilation (FGM), still goes on in remote areas of the republic. This is a fact especially within the aforementioned communities who would not compromise their cultural values or take nos for answers. The diets, hygiene, body chemistry, and how the overall nerves responded to the "cut" was/is key to timely wound healing.

The homemade young warriors were housed exclusively in temporary quarters, supervised by veteran warriors, and overseen by a senior elder within the community. The whole idea was to monitor the healing progress and confront likely incidents of emergencies and extraordinary side effects tactfully. Herbal medicines were available to handle incidental occurrences and were effective. Some herbal brands are real punchy. They cut through the healing nerves like a toothache. Extended use could be harmful to the organ being treated, so the use of the chemical was timed and carefully monitored.

For most part, no fatalities were reported, and the healing rate from a random standpoint was actually 99 percent effective. In modern times, especially in South Africa, reports have emerged whereby village circumcisers used contaminated surgery tools and contagiously spread the germs (virus) from one victim to another. Huge parks of boys had to be rushed to local hospitals for further medical treatment.

Nonetheless, scattered fatalities have been reported in quite a number of societies that still harbor the traditional cut practices. According to the best of my knowledge, quite a number of other tribes in Kenya have only male circumcision, others cut both male and female, and some minority tribes do not circumcise at all.

Amazingly, despite the grueling encounters, myself and at least twothirds of my age-mates aged late seventies and early eighties are still alive and well today.

Finally, let me alert the reader that the extent of the cutting, style, and other physical concerns are purely traditional and differs from one tribal group to the other.

For example, if a seasonal candidate misses the seasonal cutoff intentionally or accidentally, the case stays open, and the postponement is infinite. The catch-up case scenario would be rather painful because both the muscles and the body tissues of the victim would have hardened or stiffened. Be reminded that the well-known Jewish custom to date is to circumcise every male child eight days after birth whether in Jerusalem or any other jurisdiction in the world. Jesus the son of God and Isaac the son of Ibrahim, including Ibrahim at almost one hundred years, underwent circumcision. During early AD, Paul, the Apostle of Jesus Christ, personally circumcised his nephew Timothy. Timothy's mother was a Jew married to a Greek.

Paul justified Timothy's circumcision on the basis that as his nephew, he would be exposed to the Jewish radicals who would likely be inquisitive concerning Timothy's manhood and purity.

Well, it worked. No confrontational incidents were ever reported. I envision that it was rather agonizing for Ibrahim and Ismail when God commanded Ibrahim that he must be cleansed in order to be the father of a great nation. Seemingly, both Ibrahim and Ismail had to painfully alternate in cutting one another at the opportune time. They were lucky—no one got sepsis or infection by God's grace.

Thus, my fellow brethren, the Merus and other tribes under the focus umbrella are going the right way—the God's way. Perhaps, it is godly to maintain God's commandments and stay clean.

Personal Note: The sound or the appearance of the described tribal practices to the readers might reflect notions of primitivism or backwardness. Nonetheless, from the perspectives of the respective communities, the customary events and practices have value, substance, and significance because they were a means of initiating boys to adults. The circumcised men were warriors that were ready to protect the homestead or go to war.

Middle and High Schooling

Following initiation, healing, and naming ceremonies, a chance of a lifetime prompted itself in January 1955. A former classmate that attended the fifth grade with me in 1953 shared that a particular middle school (Kajionduthi) in Muthambi location approximately twelve miles from my home was admitting fifth graders and had limited positions. My mother and I rushed there next day. Sadly, we got the word upon arrival that the last and final position was filled by a neighbor's kid. He had passed the exams, but the parents were unable to raise the required school fees until that day. The headmaster in that school advised us to check with the PCEA mission supervisor of schools at Chogoria, about seven miles away from home.

We were hitting the road on foot all this time. Both Mom and I showed no signs of exhaustion or desperation. We got to Chogoria late that afternoon, met the supervisor, and explained our circumstances to him including my being out of school the whole of 1953.

Actually, I let Mom present the case, hoping for some sympathy. He sympathized but offered no viable help. As a last resort, he sarcastically suggested that we try Catholic mission schools because they were slow in getting filled. I took that to imply that Catholics were less competitive. Tough luck, we thought, but we had done our best, and the day was well spent. I knew how to pray, and I asked the supervisor and my mother to join me, which they did. I asked God to bless the supervisor for providing us with advice and for providing us with strength to walk all day including the remaining fivemile journey home and please find a school for me within PCEA in Christ's name!

My mom and I journeyed quietly back home. At this point, I was a fresh warrior, not allowed to walk closely to mothers or hold a close conversation. Also, since we were approaching our neighborhoods, I stood the risk of being spotted by a familiar face or some senior warriors who might gossip and trigger disciplinary action. It is worth noting that upon healing and coming out of seclusion, the young warriors were usually placed on probation and supervised by seniors for three months. Should any negative behavioral conduct be noticed or reported, the suspect is subjected to severe disciplinary flogging processes. With that in mind, I stayed cautious and fairly distanced myself while I walked ahead of my mother.

As I branched off on the path toward our home, I saw someone riding a bike downhill. I didn't quite recognize the rider, so I continued my walk. Shortly, I heard my mom's voice shouting, "Paulo, Paulo, is this you?" and "What brings you to our area?" The bike rider responded, "Yes, it's me, Paulo!" I became curious and decided to shield myself by coffee plantations to eavesdrop on the interchange. My mother further inquired as to what he (Paulo) was doing in our area. This was early in the evening, 6:00 p.m., and we were just half a mile away from our home. Paulo explained that he had taken over as the headmaster for my former primary school and was on his way home, actually, near Chogoria from where we were returning.

My mother got so excited, narrated my school case scenario in minutes, and asked a direct question: "Do you have a spot left in class IV for my son to repeat?" Instead of answering, Paulo asked, "Where is your son now?" My mom had a loud voice, and instead of responding to Paulo's question, she called out my first name, "Kaaaaaaaaaaaaaaaaria!" I was embarrassed because of my warrior status and the fact that I wasn't far enough. So I simply hoped that no one but me heard her. I softly responded, and she ordered me, "Come here!" (*Njuu*). I have to admit that I was not in good shape. We were dusty, exhausted, sweaty, dry-lipped, hungry, and withdrawn. In my heart, though, I felt a sigh of relief, encouragement, and a potential answer to prayer. When I appeared, Mr. Paulo asked for my names, age, and mild affirmation of what Mom had already described. Paulo asked me whether I could report to school the next day and see him first thing. I responded with a thundering, "Yes! Yes! Yes!" response. So, the Lord gave me a second chance, and I jump-started my academic dream once again in January 1955.

Sadly, the devil never takes a nap. An unwanted character partially witnessed that three-way meeting on the roadside, and it cost me dearly. From a distance, an unfriendly senior warrior stood and saw me close to Mom while I was talking to Mr. Paulo, which was against the ground rules for rookie warriors. When the accusation got reported to the group that evening, I could not adequately defend myself, so I simply gave in and bravely took the punishment like a man. I was reminded of Apostle Paul's flogging and beating incidents when he took courage to defend his Christian faith. He was not ashamed of the Bible because if he was, he would be denying the resurrection of His Lord and Savior Jesus Christ. Likewise, I took courage and persevered for the sake of my education, my warrior status, and my mom.

Well, matters settled down, and I strictly embarked on schooling and focused on capitalizing on this second chance that the Almighty God had graciously granted. Within a year, I got admitted at Chogoria Christian Academy. Traditionally, the academy admitted a combined total of 140 students (35 in each class) for both boys and girls. Every boy had to have been circumcised prior to admission.

My appetite for knowledge and competitive mode enabled me to be number one (top of my class) throughout the four-year tenure. As expected, I graduated with high marks (points) and earned my first academic diploma.

PART 2

First Search for a Job

Lack of Guidance:
Who Is Who among Whom?

Everyone has to start somewhere. So, where did I begin my career? I was expected to become *a schoolteacher*, but I wasn't sure I wanted to take that career path. Technically, I was somewhat a *jack of all trades and master of none*. Following my success in basic education and equipped with a diploma/certificate, I was qualified for an entrylevel position as an agriculturalist, clerk, carpenter, nurse, surveyor, tailor, teacher, or veterinarian. Academically I had studied agriculture, English, geography, history, science, Swahili, mathematics, civil service, and government including several local languages.

Categorically, I had opted out of further full-time studies so I could take a paying job and support my economically disadvantaged peasant family. By the time I was graduating from school, my three younger siblings had not commenced first grade. Our baby brother was eight, and the sister he followed was ten. At that time, my mind was only occupied with nagging silent questions and meditations of how and when I might be able to support my family at large. By chance, I had applied to three organizations for a clerical position prior to taking the final exams at the end of school year. East African Railways and Harbours, a regional organization, was the first to respond with an invitation for an interview two hundred miles away from my village. I acknowledged, attended a one-week intensive interview, and got selected for a one-year clerical training. They had twenty-five positions to fill and selected only 25 top candidates out of 250 interviewed. By God's grace and providence, I took the fifth position overall. Admissions to other likely institutions and a few other job offers came through but were too late to make a difference.

Job Training and Advancement

My selection to train and work for the East African Railways and Harbours (EARH) led to a career path. I was convinced that I could work, give my family the needed financial support, and study privately to gain credentials that were necessary for advancement to the higher ranks within the organization. The one-year training at the Railway Training Institute moved fast. I did well in examinations, graduated, and occupied a permanent position probationary in the region, Eldoret City—two hundred miles northeast of Nairobi.

Initially, the EARH placed me in category 2 of their personnel scheme with potential for promotion through advanced administrative training. Within two years, I earned another promotion and moved to Nakuru City within the region—one hundred miles closer to Nairobi. Within another year, in 1963, I swapped positions with a colleague and returned to Nairobi headquarters. Nairobi was closer to my home—Meru County—approximately 150 miles northeast of Nairobi City. In the interim and with God's help, I trained and passed a couple of in-house courses. The accomplishment earned me my last and final promotion within the ranks of category 1 of EARH's personnel rankings. Essentially, Nairobi remained my operational base over the next nine years until the thought of pursuing further studies arose.

Workplace Friction and Conflicts

Wherever there are human beings, anticipate conflicts. Similar to conflicts among families, siblings, parents, friends, partners, neighbors, lovers—you name it—there are conflicts in public organizations. Internally, the composition of EARH personnel was quite diverse. The whites played a dominant role in general administration while the Asian and the Arab counterparts majored in supervisory roles. The Africans were jammed in third place and scrambled for whatever was unappealing to the Asian and the Arab runners-up. So the Blacks had to fight hard for a step or what was popularly known as "annual increment." Typically, secret bribes and favors of all sorts were practiced organizational-wide. Traditionally, Asians and Arabs were corrupt, immoral, and even wicked. You won't know this just by facial appearance or behavior because of their humble demeanor. But in real life, they were selfish, stingy, and corruptible. Personally having participated in the Mau Mau struggle, I identified those behavioral evils easily.

The Whites were clearly racists and prejudiced. Warning signs and labels were openly displayed, reminding those that could read that "Africans and dogs" were not welcome in certain areas (restaurants, hotels, recreational areas, and the first floor deck of the city buses). Quite something, eh! Whites hardly shook hands with Africans. Asians and Arabs were, of course, free to enter and exit at will. So instead of raising hell and being confrontational, the Africans just suffered without bitterness. Also, Africans were forbidden from wearing hats and looking straight into the face of a White man. At one time, back in the village, I recall my father taking off his hat when he noticed a vehicle coming toward our direction on a roadside close by even without seeing the driver. All vehicles were supposedly owned by Whites.

My father had learned the rule when he served as a carrier corps during the Second World War. He also had some refresher course during his six-year detention term for taking the Mau Mau oath and adopting its ideologies. During the Colonial rule, no Africans owned cars but could work as drivers. So, if you wore a hat and noticed a vehicle in motion headed your way, take off your hat to be on the safe side. If you didn't and the White driver spotted you, he'd stop, snatch the hat, and reward you with several smacks on your face without uttering a word because it was considered disrespect to the superior race.

The White folks traditionally wore hats, and so Africans could not imitate. In addition, Africans could not drink liquor, bottled beer, wine, or smoke commercial cigarettes openly. What a life! I guess that's why there are soothing words such as *perseverance* and *self-control*. Those of us that are still alive beat the odds, so to speak.

Caught in a Trap

Between my first and second year of my career with the East African Railways, I had ventured into an adult lifestyle of dating, drinking, and smoking. I was a good dancer, good-looking, and charming. In single clubs, parties, and social occasions, most ladies would offer me a dance whenever I requested. It never occurred to me that there was anything sinister about my newfound lifestyle until a Christian friend of mine noticed that I was coughing, caught a cold frequently, and my breath was stinky. When he asked me how many cigarettes I smoked per day, I answered one pack, or twenty cigarettes. He thought that was bad enough for me and voluntarily offered personal advice. On the outset, he inquired whether I was familiar with a sickness called throat cancer. I had never heard of the word *cancer* before, so I answered negatively. At this point we agreed to meet later.

Meanwhile, he gave me an assignment: (1) To find the description of the sicknesses caused by tobacco and (2) to list five advantages of smoking and the same number for disadvantages.

At the next meeting, I only had answers for smoking disadvantages and, of course, lots of information regarding the causes and effects of throat cancer. To this, I reacted by ceasing purchase and use of tobacco products pronto. By God's grace, I overcame the bad habit at an early stage. My friend and I have maintained a lasting relationship, and we are truly brothers in Christ.

PART 3

Married Life

Here Comes the Bride

By 1965, I had served the East African Railways for a solid six years (January 1960 to December 1965). I had just attained the age of 23. Physically, I felt like a man, looked like a man outwardly, and smelled like a man. I quickly realized that most of my close age-mates were engaged to get married or had tied the knot within recent months.

My father, however, had counseled me concerning hasty or incidental marriages. He provided the following categories of marriages:

1. Free choice—a woman of good character, a virtuous woman

2. Prearranged marriage—at the convenience of parents from both sides (tribal, religious, or traditional)

3. Forced marriage—elope or without consensus

4. Voluntary—consensual relationship by the couple without parental involvement

5. Incidental marriage—based on convenience, economics, circumstantial, or oops! (accidental)

In addition, he cautioned against picking up a bride from nearby, including avoidance of hooking up with next of kin or even from family allies. He reasoned that in case of quarrels and disagreements, making resolutions/reconciliations might take longer due to interference by in-laws who are likely to side with their daughter regardless of who is at fault.

Two hundred miles away from home, I became acquainted with a lady close to my age—three years younger, to be precise. She is originally from Kiambu District, born in a village called Kiambururu.

We met in Nairobi in a Methodist church during one of Sunday morning worship services. The church was a mile away from where I lived and a few blocks from where Beatrice lived. She worked for the Nairobi City Council as a kindergarten teacher near her residence.

I was introduced to her by her girlfriend, a lady I had met through her cousin. The cousin was a friend of mine and attended the same church.

The moment I realized we were both faithful Christians and were spiritually mature, mutual communication ensued, and we treated each other cordially. Her maiden name was Beatrice Wairimu Kinuthia. For the first few months, we saw each other only on Sundays at church, chatted briefly, and said goodbyes. Back then, landline phones were scarce even at work, so people met when they met. Subsequently, time permitted, and we dated for a whole year without being intimately acquainted. We mutually agreed to demonstrate the seriousness of our relationship prior to making any announcements.

She came from a Christian family background, but I did not. Actually, she was a virgin, but I was not. However, as stated earlier, at age twelve, I became the first member of my family to confess Christ as my Lord and Savior. I dare say that my faith in Christ eventually attracted my other five siblings to Christian life and were all baptized—Eunice, my older sister; Geoffrey, brother who followed me; Joyce; Flora; and Eric, our baby brother. Eventually, both parents got converted and were baptized David and Grace, respectively.

The happy couple kept their faith till God separated them in 1989 when Dad went home "to be" with his maker. My mother was widowed till 2013 when she finally left earth to join Dad in their final resting place. Beatrice and I had no doubts concerning our PCA based faith in Christ. We had resolved any opposing issues through questions and answers. When I proposed to Beatrice in mid-1966, she accepted, and we jointly arranged to tie the knot in December of that same year. Customarily, I had to present a dowry to gain the consent of her parents. Indeed, my family and friends generously supported the initiative, and I was able to meet the premarital demands of her family. Once we had the blessings from both families, we took our marriage vows at her family church (Kambui PCA Church) on December 3, 1966. She officially became Mrs. Beatrice W. Ngaine. My family sponsored the wedding reception which took place in Nairobi City that same day. Praise be to God Almighty, we have kept the faith and the sacred vows intact to date.

Successive Offsprings

Following the union, our first baby girl "Jedidah Caroline Karimi" came into the world in February 1967, and another angel "Jennifer Martha Waithira" joined us in March 1968—thirteen months apart.

By February 1970, the third angel, "JoAnne Wanja," joined the crowd, and it was about that year that the concept of family planning pierced our ears. Our financial world at the time had become real clumpy, let alone our living conditions. The five of us (full house) lived in a one-bedroom flat, and you can imagine how comfortable we were?

Unlike the US where all residential bathrooms are internal, both our toilet and the bathroom in Nairobi were outside and shared communally by six other family groups. Oh yes! Just about time to plan—more money and less family.

Dream for Further Education

It drove me nuts to realize that my wife and I had no potential to enhance our income. Our combined monthly income grossed approximately KSh 1,000 or $100 today. As mentioned earlier, my wife still worked for the Nairobi City Council as a daycare teacher, and I continued my assignment with the East African Railways as a clerical officer. These were prestigious organizations, but the salary scales were not all that great. In addition to financing our immediate needs, we were simultaneously providing occasional support for parents at both ends including tuition for my two younger siblings that I had sponsored since first grade. Oh! I almost forgot that we also had a house helper since we both worked. She slept in an adjacent room (ten feet by ten feet) that we used as a kitchen. During that time, the idea of finding a part-time job in Kenya was not a viable option nor was promotion aspects at work for any one of us. Annual or step increments were meager and had insignificant impact on our financial needs.

Preparation for Travel Documents, Including Entry Visa to the United States

During 1970, an opportunity arose for me to further my studies in the USA. A friend I had attended middle school with in Kenya was attending college in the state of California. He had returned to Kenya for a short visit and stayed with me. When I expressed my desire to pursue further studies, he was willing to assist me in the process of obtaining Form I-20—the official admission form from an accredited (allowed to admit and train foreign students) US higher learning institutions. By this time, I was into a five-year marriage with a litter of three kids—four-, three- and one-year-old. To get started, we realized that I had to sit for US standardized scholastic aptitude test (SAT). This was a prerequisite for obtaining admission. There were no shortcuts. So I hurriedly studied for the exam, took the test, and passed. My friend, then back in America, was so impressed with the results. Equipped with this information, he conveniently obtained the admission papers for me including sponsorship documents for ease of getting a visa. Obtaining a Kenyan passport was another hassle, but by God's grace, I got it anyway. The final phase called for raising a one-way airfare in the tune of KSh 7,000 or $700. Money was slow to come by at the time. Several fundraising parties only brought in half of the airfare. Ironically, the US embassy could not issue visas without proof of fully paid airfares. The admission Form I-20 mandated that I report to college the first week of September 1971. My desperate plan B was to borrow the shortfall portion of the airfare from a couple of my favorite relatives—uncle and a cousin.

When they committed, I hastily tendered a twenty-four-hour special notice in lieu of thirty days to my employer, bought an air ticket, and rushed to the US embassy to apply for a visa. Out of the blue, at the embassy, I was informed that I needed clearance from the Ministry of Education regarding the need to study overseas. Up until then I was not aware of the requirement, and I just got shocked. I prayed for strength and guidance. God led me to an angel-lady in the Ministry of Education by the name of Mrs. Githinji. She initiated an interview that I attended timely. At the close of the interview, I could sense her concern and the desire to assist me given the urgency of the matter.

She ushered me to the waiting area and promised she would be back shortly. When she returned, she handed me an envelope addressed to the US counselor, gave me a few words of advice, and wished me luck. Time had run out for me to return to the embassy that day, so I pushed the event to the next day. The next day came, and I returned to the embassy. In the final phase of the interview, another monster struck. The US embassy needed proof that I had $300 in travelling checks to cater for any unforeseen emergencies. I had only $100 but needed $200 more. The real problem was there was no other money elsewhere. I did not want to panic or create suspicion that I wasn't ready to provide the needed proof. In good faith, I asked to be excused to go to the bank and get the additional money. Just by coincidence, I remembered that my colleague and a friend had applied and received an academic loan that week that he didn't have to spend right away. I reasoned with him that if he'd advance me the equivalent of $200, I would present the money order to the US embassy and get the visa. Once the visa matter was settled, I'll cash the traveler's checks, give his money back, and we'd be back to square one. I sounded like a conman, but the formula worked. I got the visa that same day! We praised God and celebrated like good old buddies. Harrison remained my dear friend. He also let me keep $10 as pocket money just in case.

We maintained a brotherly relationship until 1998 when a terrorist bomb in Nairobi took his life that year. He owned and operated a property management company in a building across the street from the US embassy. The entire building was tragically flattened, and there were no survivors. May God bless and save his soul for eternity.

Resignation from My First Job

As noted above, I tendered my twenty-four-hour resignation from my first job in mid-October 1971 to pursue further academic studies in the United States of America. Despite serving the EARH for eleven years, the terms of my employment did not allow me to receive any benefits besides earned annual leave. I had to serve for twenty-five years or attain the age of fifty-five years to vest the benefits. Ironically, I met none of those requirements. Simply put, I just broke even—no gain no loss.

First Separation from Family

This was about to be my first air flight ever and a day of mixed emotional separation for the family. Our third-born, Joanne, only twenty-two months old at the time, was left at home asleep under the watch of my sister Flora. Flora was living with us while she attended a day high school in Nairobi, and she was assisted by the housemaid. Her name was Betty. My wife and the older girls accompanied me to a midnight flight from Nairobi to London via Paris, France. A few relatives and friends accompanied us to the airport.

Following the send-off prayers by a family friend (John Njeru), I just took off without any more hugs and kisses. I doubt the kids had any clue regarding their dad's destination. I noticed scattered sobs here and there, but that was it. Within an hour, I was airborne to London. The family never met again until mid-July 1976 when half of us reunited.

Details of how we got reunited are narrated in the later pages of this book. Meanwhile, while I struggled with life and pursuance of better knowledge in an entirely strange country, my wife struggled keeping her job with the Nairobi City Council and the challenges of raising and protecting three young children in an urban environment alone. Quite a number of negative events blocked our paths, but we continued our walk of faith, prayed intensely, and persevered through countless hardships. By the grace of God, we overcame. My wife was naturally gifted with hospitality, thrift, patience, kindness, self-discipline, and focus.

Later on, through working part-time, I found a way of sending her regular financial help, and that alone alleviated social hurdles off her shoulders. Likewise, I had taken my sister that lived with us prior to my departure to a boarding school and assisted my parents financially back in the village. In addition, we all communicated through letters, greetings through friends, and occasional landline phone calls. This mode of life continued throughout the period of separation.

PART 4

Migration to the United States of America

Arrival in the US Capital—
Washington DC

My life story in America starts here. I landed in Washington DC, USA, on November 21, 1971. Two weeks earlier, I had bought a one-way air ticket in Nairobi, Kenya, and flew Pan Am Airlines via Heathrow Airport in London. En route, I stopped over in London for a week to visit a colleague of mine (James Gichoga) with my former employer, East African Railways and Harbours. He was in London for a one-year job-related training. Even though I travelled through London a few times later on, that was the last time I had the opportunity to visit the inner surroundings. London is an ancient city. As such, building structures are monumental, landmarks, and historical. Without a desire to shop around or sightseeing, London could be lonely and boring.

Actually just realizing that this was the central business center of a former Colonial master, there was a sudden sentiment of psychological turnoff. I got reminded of demoralizing signs I mentioned earlier such as "Africans and dogs are prohibited" around New Stanley Hotel along Kenyatta Avenue in downtown Nairobi. Soon after Kenya became independent in early December 1963, the signs disappeared. When I visited Kenya in 1988, I inquired about my friend's whereabouts only to learn that he had passed on. He and I had started our careers the same year (1960) and had shared some good and bad times during the colonial era.

I landed at Dulles International Airport, Virginia, USA, just a day before the famous last Thursday of November, popularly known as Thanksgiving. My cousin George welcomed me with both hands and gave me a temporary accommodation. He was one of the guests at a friend's thanksgiving dinner, and so I accompanied him. I had a great time watching the American football for the first time and tasting turkey meat and Budweiser beer in a can. Having grown up in the same environment in Kenya, he and I share similar sentiments, identical processes including cultural upbringing. We were both initiated into manhood traditionally just two years apart (1952 and 1954, respectively). We shared a one-bedroom apartment in Northwest DC and lived harmoniously until he got married a few years later. We both now reside in the state of Maryland, we are US citizens, relate well to each other, and always there for each other.

Each of us have four children—just by coincidence.

College Education in the US

In the interim, the notion of moving to California had drastically changed. Through inquiries, I realized that the state of economy in that state was not all that accommodating to foreign students and, further, that local transportation would be quite a challenge.

After some consultations and discussion with cousin George and other Kenyan associates, we decided to relocate to DC by seeking admission to another international school in the area. When I presented the new official Form I-20 with some mild justification, the Department of Immigration and Naturalization Services graciously approved and authorized the transfer. This change of events was quite a relief considering that I was three months late in reporting to my college of initial admission. Following this change, I became part of the Kenyan population in Washington DC. I continued living with my beloved cousin George while attending my amateur Blackwell School of Business in the US capital.

The Academic Struggle

Up until my enrollment at Blackwell Business College in January 1972, I hadn't sat in a class since 1968 when I had taken an in-house refresher course with my former employer. In the finals, I had emerged as one of the best students in class and was rewarded with an ink pen.

Everyone in class cheered for me, and I felt great. In the middle of that month (March 14), my wife and I had celebrated the birth of our second daughter. To me it felt like a double fortune. At the end of that year, my employer later rewarded me with a huge raise. Now, four years later, here I was—a student in a higher learning institution all over again. At any rate, the tune-up got me going through freshman classes with ease. I found the declaration of a major a unique challenge to foreign students due to massive career choices. After the first year in college, the academic path kind of lit up for me. Except for the electives, I strictly pursued business-related courses. Within two years, I earned my first college diploma, an associate in business administration (ABA). Immediately, I enrolled at the University of the District of Columbia (UDC), a four-year college, and majored in accounting.

Early Jobs while in College: Are You Hiring?

Having worked in Kenya for eleven years as a civil servant, as noted earlier, I had adequate practical and real-life experience in human relations, teamwork, self-discipline, morale, and survival techniques such as *ropes to know* and *ropes to skip*. My cousin George, who had pioneered into the US two years earlier, had, by chance, pre-educated me by sharing his newly gained experiences that readiness, flexibility, honesty, physical wellness, and self-confidence were integrals to survival as a self-sponsored student in the US. Incidentally, both of us were active in "Boy Scouts" organization events in Kenya and had learned the scouts' motto, which is to always "be prepared"!

Understandably, I did not have any form of health insurance, but God covered me with His grace. I was fairly healthy and immune to some contagious viruses. Equipped with this handpicked "arsenal," I was ready for both economic and academic war.

Instantaneously, a friend of my cousin George named Moses, a fellow Kenyan who lived in the same building and eventually became my friend, knew a colleague of his that owned a small moving company and needed a few handymen off and on. On my first Saturday of that Thanksgiving week, the company needed five such helpers.

When I expressed interest, Moses called the man, and he hired me on the phone even prior to meeting me. I worked for the company successfully for three months. Subsequent assignments were as follows:

1. In January 1972, another Kenyan friend (Simon) helped me get a job as a night Securicor/desk, clerk/receptionist all in one at $1.75 per hour. By the time I moved on to the next job, I was making $2.25 per hour working from 4:00 p.m. to twelve midnight.

2. To supplement the income, another Kenyan friend (Makumi), a chef, got me a part-time spot as a busboy working on the weekends, holidays, and school breaks.

3. In June 1974, another Kenyan friend (Mbote) assisted me to secure a night garage cashier/manager position that paid me $3.25 an hour. During this time, I was a full-time self-sponsored student, supporting my wife and three kids in Kenya, including my parents. I kept this job until my wife and the youngest daughter joined me in June 1976 and continued through August 1978 when I resigned to pursue graduate studies at The University of Hartford in Connecticut. I earned $3.50 per hour by the time I exited.

4. While enrolled in a full-time graduate program at the University of Hartford (UH) in 1979 to 1980, I applied for a chef's assistant position posted on the notice board at the UH campus. The position was at the Catholic seminary in Hartford, Connecticut, close to the university. I followed up by a phone call and got invited for an interview. Well,

it turned out I was the only candidate, and I was hired on the spot. The chef and I cooked for 150 students and a fifteen-member staff daily. I retained this job till May 1981, when I finally graduated from UH.

Graduation, Training, and Advancement

In 1978, I graduated cum laude from the University of the District of Columbia with a bachelor of business administration (BBA), in accounting. In addition, I earned a master of science in professional accounting (MSPA) from the University of Hartford, Connecticut, in 1981. These accomplishments added a layer of popular academic credentials to my name for career purposes. Subsequently, over the years, I topped these credentials with an additional layer of certifications: certified public accountant (CPA) in 1993 and chartered global management accountant (CGMA) in 2012.

By the grace of God, the tuition pathway in the three institutions I attended got softened miraculously: (1) At Blackwell College, I was awarded the president's one-year free scholarship for academic achievement and outstanding leadership qualities. Incidentally, I had volunteered for an opening prayer in a college event when a designated person failed to attend due to an emergency. The impromptu act caught the president's attention, and we stayed close. (2) At the University of the District of Columbia, a residency law changed and allowed recognition of any resident students domiciled in DC to pay a minimum fee of only $70 for a full semester's load regardless of the state of origin or country. I was a DC resident then, so I became an instant beneficiary. (3) The University of Hartford granted me onehalf of annual tuition based on my undergraduate GPA and the fact that I was a minority student. The Kenyan Ministry of Education took care of the remaining one-half plus boarding, and I only took care of books and supplies. In fact, this was a remarkable financial relief.

My student status after graduate studies had categorically staggered, and I was "out of status." For once, I was unable to decide whether or not to return my new talents back to Kenya, pursue a terminal degree (PhD), or seek permanent stay in the US. While I wrestled with these uncertainties, I continued earning a living for my immediate family by adopting a philosophy I had learned privately, which is that "if you have a job, save it till you land on another job, but if you don't have a job…your job is to look for a job without bias!" Since I did not have a job, I was off to the open job market.

Search for Employment—
Second Time Around

1. In the spring of 1981, I accepted a temporary sales position and worked as a car salesman for a Toyota company in Maryland on commission "only" basis. The Toyota Camrys, mini pickups, and the Corollas had just landed into the market and were selling like "hotcakes." To the best of my recollection, my highest commission checks ranged between $1,800 and $2,500 per week. Six months into the trade, I felt uncomfortable doing this for long when I realized that the consumers were paying too much for overpriced commodities. These tricks are nicknamed "trade secrets." Hence, I walked away peacefully.

2. During 1982, I served as a commercial driving school instructor for a local school. My specific role was teaching driving laws and rules to high school "learner drivers" age 16 and above in a classroom followed by on-the-road practices. Despite a minimal pay of $9 per hour, I had permission to keep and use the vehicle that I used for road instructions and practice for personal use. In addition, I was intrigued by the fact that I was making young drivers safe on the road and helping the community with roadsafety issues. The flexibility enabled me to train my wife to obtain her valued driver's license. However, I moved on when I realized that the owners were not eager to consider a raise or profit sharing. When I initially inquired, the owner simply uttered, "No time soon!"

3. In 1987, a Kenyan friend (Dr. Manyara) that worked for the MCI phone company learned of the company's plan to hire more accountants. He arranged for my interview with his manager. After the fact, I was on the job within a week. I settled for a $12 an hour deal for a start. I graciously served for a year. During December of 1987, MCI lost a monopoly-related case in court. AT&T had sued MCI on a monopoly-related issue and won a money judgment.

Consequently, MCI was forced to downsize its personnel including relocation to another state. The shakeup affected my position, and I was inevitably released (laid off) on a "last in first out" (LIFO) basis inventory scheme. The job was quite fascinating. I reviewed and processed vendor invoices (accounts payable) to the tune of $999,000 per day cumulatively, five days a week.

The subsequent advanced career undertakings were adjunct faculty followed by associate professor at the University of the District of Columbia, associate professor at Southeastern University in DC until I joined the US Federal Government in 2003.

PART 5

Family Reunion

Reunion with Spouse and Third Daughter in the US

I was still enrolled at UDC as a junior student when in the summer of 1976, an American friend I had met in social setups privately realized that I had left my immediate family (wife and three kids) back in Kenya when I travelled to the US in late 1971. Concerned about the "noble" separation, my friend felt he could organize some form of sponsorship that would secure visas for my wife and the baby to join me. Through inquiries, we learned that US Immigration Form-F2 was valid for requesting visas for spouses and children of full-time students of which I was one. Well, we applied, and by God's grace, my wife and the third daughter, who was six years then, were issued visas to join me in the US. The memorable event took place in July 1976—almost five years since I had left Kenya.

Consequently, we placed the two older ones in a boarding school and designated one of our sisters (Aunt Esther) to oversee their welfare, including upkeep during school breaks and holidays. Thank God all went well.

In September of 1976, my wife was offered an office assistant job by the Kenyan embassy in DC, which she gladly accepted. Two years later in the summer of 1978, we became aware that my wife could change her status from F-2 (a dependent of a student) to an A-2 status. The A-2 visa provided a diplomatic status and entitled the respective holder to petition the change of immigration status for his/ her immediate dependents. The size of such dependents was never an issue. The occasion opened an immediate window for our two girls back in Kenya to join us. Sure enough, when my wife requested the change, the US Department of State approved, and their travel visas were issued pronto. The girls were in the US by early August 1978.

Despite their typical rookie-day challenges, everyone eventually got assimilated and got fairly adjusted to daily chores.

Graduate Studies and Second Separation from Family

Following graduation from UDC in June 1978, I reluctantly applied for a minority scholarship at the University of Hartford for a master of science in professional accounting (MSPA) in the fall of 1978. I never followed up on the application until an admission letter came through from the university in late July congratulating me and all the good stuff. There it was—an opportunity for me to attend graduate school almost for free!

I was faced with three major fronts: First, quit my job in DC; second, pursue graduate studies; and third, abandon my newly reunited family with only my wife's income. Given that the children in Kenya had just been issued travel visas, my wife and I resolved to postpone conclusive decisions until the girls arrived. Things were happening so fast that when we got word that the girls had obtained the entry visas, they were in US in a week. Finally, we were reunited as a family since November 1971. We jointly celebrated by shedding tears of joy for one another. Within the next week, we were at the table, reviewing the final touches on the graduate school project.

This was a tough one for all of us. The kids said nothing. We simply informed them of our unanimous decision—that dad will go for further studies with immediate effect but will be calling every other day, visit monthly, and spend holidays and school breaks together. I had not seen or been with these kids for seven years in a row. Finally, here they are, and off I go. It was hard for all of us, but we had to play our respective roles. We had the courage and mutual determination. We all understood that these were joint sacrifices that would cater for our better tomorrow.

Thank goodness that the older kids had already gotten used to sudden separations, so the going away was not a total shock. They took it lightly now that their mom and baby sister were in the loop. The hardest part, though, was when we prayed the day I took off to New England. As we all said amen, Jedi, the oldest daughter, sobbed. Her sisters joined in, and, finally, their mom. I hugged them in a pile, and while rushing out to the car, I, too, sobbed badly. Soon I gained control, and I drove off alone, headed north on a 165-mile-long road I had not travelled before. GPS was not in effect then. I used a road map. It took me five hours to reach my destination. I called the house from a payphone and talked to each one of them. That call was like a dessert after dinner for all of us. Laughters of joy echoed at both ends. Thank God that in the long run, we all succeeded and were encouraged. God is great!

Birth of Our Last Child in the US

Our last-born daughter was born on March 23, 1979. Customarily, we named her Njeri after my wife's older sister. She is a real American by birth. I was on my first year graduate program at the University of Hartford in Connecticut. I took a week off from school just to welcome her into the world. This happened during the midterms, so I had to play catch-up, anyway. Out of the blues, the doctors had to perform a C-section to get her out. Her mom is five feet tall with a normal weight of less than 130 pounds. At 7.4 pounds, the kid was a bit heavy for a normal delivery. In less than ten days, we were home, and Njeri continued to grow in stature, knowledge, and wisdom.

Academically, she has earned a master of science (MS) degree in public health. Her undergraduate degree was a BS in chemistry. Njeri is well liked, admired, and respected by her colleagues and friends.

Except for Jennifer who suddenly departed from earth at age forty-one, the rest of the offsprings are alive and well and stay united.

Family and friends remember Jennifer fondly and so many other sweet memories. All are college graduates and have added five promising grandchildren to the family tree—four granddaughters and one grandson. Our oldest granddaughter has already earned a bachelor of science degree in biology and intends to pursue a career in gynecology.

Struggle with US Immigration

First Change of US Immigration Status

Following graduation from graduate studies, I had run out of status with US immigration laws in the spring of 1981. I could have had my F-1 student visa status extended for one more year provided I had a job offer for one year from an American company for practical purposes. I did not have such an offer, so I maintained a low profile. I was illegally in the country for a good nine months when an attorney that I had consulted with asked me whether I had any relatives working for an embassy. Of course, I was aware that when my wife joined me in the US in 1977, she joined the Kenyan embassy as a local staff and had recently earned an A-2 visa status. I affirmatively answered yes! He asked who, and I replied, "My wife." He responded with, "You know, Rachi, your problem is solved!" I asked, "How?" Then he explained that my wife's status as an A-2 visa holder entitled her to obtain visas for her immediate family members, which obviously included me and our two children that we obtained visas for three years ago. Problem solved indeed. However, since my F-1 student visa had expired, the immigration rule was that I had to get out of the US and reenter the country with a different new visa status. Canada, instead of Kenya, became the wisest option. A colleague of my wife at the Kenyan embassy arranged for me to travel to Ottawa, Canada, to effect the change. I successfully made the trip and returned to US afresh within a week.

God always works in miraculous ways. God never fails! I ended up earning the status of an A-2 visa holder.

Second Change of US Immigration Status

There is an old saying that goes like this: "A change is as good as a rest." In 1988, during the reign of US president Ronald Reagan, an immigration law was enacted that allowed aliens (foreigners) who had entered the US legally prior to December 31, 1971, had not travelled outside US except for brief emergencies, and had proof of where they had lived or living, had no criminal record, and had filed their taxes timely could apply for a change of status to "green card" (permanent residency). Well, I obtained a copy of the written law from the government press. When I realized I met all the prerequisite criteria, I personally completed the application and mailed it in.

Within a month I was called for an interview, and in just another month, I had the green card in my hands. The resulting change of status paved the way in July 1988 for me, my wife, and our youngest daughter, Njeri, aged nine at the time, to travel to our homeland Kenya. This was my first visit to the land since flying away seventeen years earlier. It was a real cool homecoming. That trip opened the friendly skies, and since then, I have travelled to Kenya every two years at best.

Upon return to the States, I made up my mind to jump-start preparations to become a CPA. The recent visit to Kenya had convinced me that it was rather untimely for me to migrate back to the country. First, the political climate in the country was in turmoil and risky due to Mwakenya underground movement.

Notably, intellectuals and political activists were incriminatingly targeted, arrested, and detained without trial.

Second, my wife had a job in the US that she liked and enjoyed, and, thirdly, the children had settled down and had adequately adjusted to the US school systems and the climate as well.

Furthermore, after seventeen years of absence from the country, my contacts and connections were in disarray.

Optionally, I had fairly been exposed to accounting practice including teaching. I was gaining experience and had become convinced that accountancy was the future for me and had found my calling. I was continually getting enthused and fascinated by theory and practical mechanics of the discipline. You see, accountancy is an applied science and, indeed, the language of business.

Some of the attractions were the following hearty facts:

1. No one can argue when you say, "I am the person who counts when handling issues."

2. Your debits always equal your credits.

3. You have rare durable credentials that people admire.

4. It is the only profession directly connected to life's two inevitabilities—death and taxes.

5. You can work on weekends and public holidays.

6. No one asks, "How do you spell this or that?"

7. You get all the pens and pencils you need in all colors—you name it.

8. In Scrabble, *Accountant* (10) is worth more than the *Doctor* (6) or *Lawyer* (6).

9. You get to enjoy the great indoors—well dressed.

10. You get to enjoy and experience five seasons a year: summer, fall, winter, spring, and tax.

11. You have a wardrobe of identical white shirts, matching ties, suits, and an assortment of business casuals.

12. You get to work unlimited hours unconventionally.

13. The likelihood of infinite clientele and jingles in your pocket.

14. Good accountants are *rarely* unemployed.

15. Independently, you can maintain integrity, objectivity, and stay passionate.

Final Advancement from Alien Status to US Citizenship

Transitioning to citizenship was easy. Holders of green cards can undergo this function after waiting for five years following graduation into the green card arena. Once again, criminal records, bankruptcies, and delinquency in filing tax returns are not entertained.

Finally, applicants must pass an interview, a verbal uniform civil, political, and history-related test. This takes place on the scheduled interview date. Questions are randomly drawn from a base of one hundred questions. The adjudicator/interviewer may ask any number of questions especially if you fail to provide correct answers. To prepare, I crammed all the base questions and answers, and sure enough, I scored well.

The outcomes were pronto. Following the end of the session, a hand was extended to me congratulating me for having become a naturalized US citizen by choice. This simply meant that even though I was not born on US soil, I met other equivalent standards that merited my entitlement to the status of an American citizen. Hurrah!

PART 6

A Career with the US Government

By God's providence, I had accepted a subcontractor's position with Allmond & Company CPAs (a public accounting firm) to perform accounting and analytical functions for the Drug Enforcement Administration (DEA) under the US Department of Justice. The assignment had commenced in October 2001 and was to last for four years. During the latter part of 2002, then at age sixty, an accounting position opened in the agency I worked under. Well, I applied, and to my surprise, I interviewed and got selected. I got the offer and accepted even without alerting my immediate employer—the Allmond & Company. The requirement for separation between me and the company was that either party could give two weeks' notice of intent to separate, and that was exactly what I did.

I got started with the US Federal Government effective March 8, 2003. From that day, at age sixty-one, I had officially become a civil servant for the world's greatest country.

US Civil Service and Duration

I graciously served the US government as an accountant, auditor, and programs inspector for fifteen years.

Workplace Frictions—Two at Work

During my first year of service as a civil servant, I realized that unlike the professional public accounting sector, professional qualifications for government employees were minimal. For example, a supervisor/ manager in a finance department needed only twenty-four credit hours in accounting and did not need a college degree or diploma. In addition, the government had adopted a policy of prioritizing veteran applicants who met basic criteria for certain positions that required minimum skills. In essence, such a hiring process gives the appearance of nepotism and evils of superiority complex mentalities. For example, when my new family of colleagues became aware that I was a CPA (certified public accountant) and had two advanced college degrees, they became envious and antagonistic. Not for the reason that I would jeopardize anyone's position or progress, but may be for general phobia such as humiliations, intimidations, etc. In particular, the section chief in my department had a bachelor's degree and was a CPA. However, for reasons unknown to me, every part of my work-product became a threat to the chief. At one point, I drafted a memo for the administrator that he was unable to develop. When my "draft memo" was received by the deputy assistant administrator (DAA), the overall chief. The draft was immediately approved, hailed, and made part of permanent departmental reference (go-by) materials. Apparently, it became clear that the chief and I were further distanced, and nothing ever changed. Having felt the tension of the resentment to my throat, I requested and was granted a lateral transfer to another office.

While you serve, there are things/matters you must know and/ or skip. Based on the learning curve, both in private sector and now inside the government, I resolved not to get involved in the following:

- Not to be confrontational in a work environment

- Not to seek a supervisory/leadership position in a sensitive environment

- Not to publicize personal matters, interests, opinions, or thoughts

- Not to gossip or share secrets

- Not express political or religious affiliations, personal problems, likes, or dislikes

- Not to provoke, be outspoken, or be an activist

- Not to seek favors or preferences

- Not to be nosy or a whistleblower

- Not to insubordinate or be critical

- Maintain social skills, positive attitude, coolness, self-control, and low profile

- Ropes to know and ropes to skip

Instead, I opted to be professional, independent, a role model, supportive, dependable, trustworthy, reliable, and a team player. In any event, I made it clear to my counterparts that I deserved the right to agree/disagree with any issue that I believed was not in accord and out of line with what I believed to be absolute truth and factual based on circumstances and context.

My transformed personality within the world's greatest civilization enabled me to realize that within the government there is bureaucracy, a system of governance that operates in a unique way whereby the system silently tolerates abuse of power, bigotry, belittling, cheating, concealment, coverup, cynicism, demeanor, dishonesty, discrimination, envy, favoritism, fraud, hatred, hypocrisy, ignorance, infighting, innuendos, jealousy, lies, mockeries, naivety, nepotism, pretense, profiling, racism, sarcasm, scandals, skepticism, secrets, segregation, suspicion, theft, and so forth.

As a professional, I quickly learned that the government is a bureaucracy founded on political dimensions of democracy; a government of the people, formed by the people, to serve the people. Hence, the majority of the leadership group such as directors and administrators are political appointees. Incidentally, 90 percent of the workforce is composed of friends, relatives, associates, or political supporters. The academic requirements for the hires are basically minimal (e.g., high school diploma or equivalent, college diploma/ degree, an occupational certificate, or some special experience/training).

The remaining 10 percent of the pie is monopolized by contractors, subcontractors, or consultants. This percentage of the workforce performs all the professional aspects of government workload.

The measurement tool for performance is *effectiveness* and not necessarily *efficiency*!

The annual evaluation criteria for productivity are

1. outstanding

2. excellent

3. satisfactory

Any of these scores qualifies an employee for a raise, promotion, or an award.

The evaluations are basically subjective since there are no specific workloads for gauging the quality of performance objectively.

The key factor is attendance without regard to productivity.

Permanent employees are required to put in eight hours per day or forty hours per week and are paid biweekly (eighty hours per pay period). Permanent employees do not sign in or out. Temporary and contractors are required to sign in. Some full-time workers are away from their desks all day or for weeks at times, and only the supervisor or close associates know their whereabouts. The recently adopted telework scheme is another added benefit to the workforce, especially parents of school-age children. They are supposedly working from home for three days (twenty-four paid hours) without any mandatory requirement to support the work done electronically or otherwise. It is a simple trust system. Annual leave, sick leave, emergencies, and official travels are exercised online or via telephones. Abuses of all sorts are rampant. Typically, there is no close supervision of anyone, and double-checks are limited. Lunch breaks are typically thirty minutes, are taken randomly, and there are no enforcements. Likewise, coffee, stretch-outs, and smoke breaks are set for fifteen minutes, but again, no enforcements are in place. The flexibility is terribly abused.

Most of the supervisors are laybacks or nonconfrontational for fear of lawsuits, antagonism, and internal frictions. Outbursts are rare, but gossips are cultural.

Civil servants are a unique category of the national workforce that is so secure. The law protects everyone without regard to color, creed, gender, sex orientation, national origin, age, disability, race, or religion. Despite differences in skin colors, we are created equal.

However, severe discipline cases have resulted in dismissals, imprisonments, demotions, fines, deferred step increments, transfers, reassignments, castigations, resignations, or early retirements.

Based on this awareness, some civil servants are inevitably accusers, antagonists, blamers, complainants, phony, gossipers, idlers, informers, intimidators, investigators, nosy, pretenders, sloppy, slanders, spies, whistleblowers, etc.

Some of them suffer from agony, agitation, complexes (inferiority/superiority), insanity, deadlocked, desperations, discouragement, frustrations, isolated, lonely, trapped, and wishful thinking.

In civil service, there is no mandatory retirement age, health, or physical prerequisites. Notably, the handicaps from all walks of life make up a sizable component of the government workforce. Also, veterans are a preferred domain for filling government-related positions where applicable. Some announcements for open positions are very specific (e.g., "Veterans only").

Travelling US-Wide and Globally

My job assignment at the Department of Justice provided me with a rare privilege and opportunity to visit places I had never dreamed of or imagined. These were places where people might not have hesitated to visit and even migrate to if they had a chance. My official travel roster in my roles as an accountant, auditor, and inspector enabled me to travel six times a year to major US key states and cities including capitals of foreign countries in six continents except Australia. To me, I did not recognize any significant historical difference between the UK and Australia—so I purposely avoided assignments that would have taken me there. I prayed, and God granted my wish.

While on travel, I lodged in five-star hotels and resorts for five to seven nights a week sometimes—for three weeks in a row. I travelled around the world one and a half times and covered hundreds of thousands of miles. I visited historical sceneries, tourist attractions, monuments, collected souvenirs, met and greeted local residents, and tasted their traditional cuisines. I feasted on popular cuisines but not everything on the menu. Nothing reacted negatively. On all these travel voyages, Lord forbade, there was not a single emergency, loss of luggage, sickness, or mishap.

There were minor time delays, of course, but that was part of the travel menu. The Lord made it all well for me. I will be grateful forever.

I believe God set me up by His divine providence to see and witness what goes on around the globe and how peoples of different cultures, civilizations, and sporadic economic systems cope with day-to-day challenges despite trials and tribulations including pain and sufferings.

Call It Quits

Toward the end of fiscal year 2016, I developed mixed feelings regarding the need for furtherance of my career with the federal government. Having travelled the world over, one and one-half times (already noted earlier), it became apparent that future travel assignments would be duplications of performances and revisitations of worksites previously covered. Personally, I was no longer enthused about future journeys nationally or internationally. In addition, having experienced the discriminative civil culture of *whom* you know vis a vis *what* you know during rare occasions of promotions and advancements, I convinced myself that the position I held was my last. At step 9 out of 10 within my grade series, I had climaxed my potential, and I was turning seventy-four in December.

Just for the fun of it and as a last resort, I resolved into attempting the following:

1. Seek a lateral movement within the agency—a common exercise government-wide (i.e., move to a different office in the same position/rank).

2. 2. Relocate to the agency's foreign office in another country.

3. 3. Retire within twelve months if nothing materialized.

Well, I tried, but nothing materialized. Accordingly, I officially gave written notice at the beginning of fiscal year 2018 of my intention to retire from my full-time position of Inspector of Programs in the Office of Inspector General within the Department of Justice in the US Federal Government. The planned decision gave me a rare sigh of relief and a real peace of mind. I specifically requested that the retirement be made effective one week following my seventy-fifth birthday. The request was granted, and my career journey ended in jubilation! The official retirement date on the records is January 6, 2018. All is well that ends well! Truly, my active career journey ended well.

PART 7

Mentors, Influencers, and Inspirers

"Giving a credit where it is due" is a common saying in real-life situations.

- My father, David Ngaine, and my mother, Grace Ngaine, deserve lots of credit for rearing and bringing me up in the early forties with zero money down. My parents were highly motivated and worked tirelessly. They showered me with rich advice, counsel, and wisdom. My dad's special advice when he said to me, "Keep your secrets secretive and memorize your personal defenses" is still crystal clear in my mind. Except for a six-acre ancestral land, 150 coffee plants, and a handful of domestic animals, the family had no other sources of wealth. Nonetheless, I matured to school and adult age with provisions of basic needs—food, shelter, love, and a sense of belonging.

- Special recognition and positive memories of the village council of elders that coached, disciplined, mentored, and educated teenage boys on various levels of cultural norms, history, customs, and societal values.

- My grade school teacher (headmaster), Mr. Peter Manene, for teaching me basic math, grammar, reading, writing, and communication skills.

- My middle school teachers: Eustace Mutegi (math teacher), who disclosed to me that mathematics was just another language—a numbers game. Alexander Kiraithe (English teacher), who emphasized that if one could speak a language, read and write in that language; "they are learned." Eustace Raagu (history teacher), who reminded students that history is based on past events (e.g., Yesterday is history today. Those events' dates, locations, and characters do not change). He emphasized that recollections, narratives, or notations were essential.

- Gerald Njagi (woodwork teacher) and Epentus Mbae (joinery teacher). Both agreed that the appearance of a good product, art, furniture or a painting, handwriting, silently talked for the producer. Incidentally, one of my supervisors at my first job often commended my written work by noting that it was impeccable.

- Another first career supervisor, Sergio Collassol, who advised me to pursue professional accounting, financial management, or economics noting that they would stabilize my chosen career path.

- Stanley Gathigira—an early days' writer and publisher. He was spectacular in writing and publishing vernacular reading materials for early scholars, first grade through fourth.

"Muthoomere" (*Reader's Digest*), "Ng'ano" (*Fairy Stories*), and "Maundu Ma Tene-Tene" (*The Ancient Days*) were among the rankings. These were my first readings ever in lower classes, and I was turned on just like in electricity.

Amazingly, I archived some quotes from those early readings that I love reciting.

- Carey Francis, BA, MA; educator, writer, and publisher— He published textbooks in mathematics, geography, social studies, etc. His inspiring texts were academically utilized in middle and high schools all over East Africa during my time. He inspired me to pursue a master's degree credential.

- Taita Arap Towett, MA, PhD, educator and public Servant. Dr. Towett's view on academic success was that academic success should be based on effective learning and passing of standardized exams and not necessarily on A and B grade schemes. To prove a point, Dr. Towett earned his two advanced degrees in linguistics and culture while working full-time and feeding a huge family of over twenty members.

He reinforced my belief that "with God and opportunity, all things are possible."

- Bernard Mate, BA. Mr. Mate was the first college graduate in my home area (Meru County) in the early 1950s.

Actually, he was one of the first eight (8) members of Legislative Council (Leg-Co) in Kenya during the Colonial era back in 1957. He had graduated with honors in history from Cambridge University in London. We had gotten acquainted with each other from social perspectives in Nairobi and occasional appearances at community-based events. In fact, I had sought a last-minute advice from him in mid-1971; soon I learned that I would be travelling abroad. By coincidence, I got word that he was hosting an event in a nearby restaurant close to my home. When we got to talk, he advised me against majoring in social sciences such as history or geography but instead to focus on thought-provoking modern ideologies of high tech, math/ science, and business-related courses (finance and economics).

Accounting was not popular at the time. When I visited Kenya in 1988 after a seventeen-year absence, I had planned to look him up and share my overseas experiences and accomplishments with him. Sadly, however, I learned that the pioneer graduate had passed on naturally a few years earlier. I simply prayed that the Almighty God would preserve his soul for eternity.

- My former undergraduate professors—George Wiley, Erol Salmon, and Dr. Buck. All were from minority back grounds but fully equipped with academic and CPA credentials.

Their heartfelt advice was inspiring to me and other minority accounting students. They emphasized pursuance of postgraduate studies and eventual certification in public accounting.

- My graduate school professor—Professor Goodman—who constantly reminded me not to lose sight of solidifying my accounting credentials to the level of certified public accountant (CPA). Incidentally, I was the only minority student in his class. He simply put it, "To succeed as an accountant, become a CPA."

- My professional counterparts—Dr. Symon Manyara, Abdul Karim, and Marvin Almond, CPAs. As a rookie in the profession, they mentored and coached me regarding preparing and taking professional exams. They emphasized that self-confidence, persistence, and stamina were integrals. In addition, they placed emphasis on integrity, ethics, and professional objectivity. I have observed these guidelines continually. These guidelines still play a role in my day-to-day life endeavors.

- Finally, the one and only Black American president, Barack H. Obama, from 2008–2016. He personally inspired me with his humane demonstration of courage, competence, audacity, perseverance, self-confidence, self-determination, stamina, work excellence and ethics, and guidance through the thorny paths of self-identification, class, and race. Of course, we can. "Yes, we can!" From a self-esteem perspective, the former president impressed that "without believing in-self, one cannot accomplish much."

Other Significant People in My Life

- My recruiter into the Federal Government—Mr. Richard Kay, Deputy Assistant Administrator, and a host of colleagues and associates. When he hired me, Mr. Kay remarked that he had a rare opportunity to hire the only foreign-born CPA in his thirty-two-year civil service.

- Mr. David Lee, owner of Empress Restaurant in Washington, DC. Mr. Lee allowed me to eat and drink anything on the house menu in appreciation of the hospitality and courtesy I extended the patrons to his new restaurant when I worked as a night manager for an area parking garage while still a full-time student between 1975 to 1978. He also recognized my hard work at school as a foreign student for he had two sons that had no desire for college education. Being a foreigner himself, he cherished the fact that "*hard work leads to real success in life.*"

Most of the mentors encouraged me to exploit my fullest potential in all of my undertakings. I did that by applying a common philosophy of "doing good until the good became better and the better best." There is a general consensus that once anyone does their best under given circumstances, that is all they can do. I believe I did not let anyone down. I did my best! Now at age 77, I feel strong mentally, physically, and spiritually. I have been blessed by the *best*!

PART 8

Retirement Life

I would categorically state without hesitation that "Retirement is truly a rare gift from God!" When I finally laid down my trade tools, it felt like a miracle. Not too many people retire formally. Folks have been forced into retirement by sickness, death, injury, discipline, incompetence, and numerous bitter and untimely circumstances.

Looking back, I realized that I had worked continuously except for weekends, holidays, and vacations since January 1960. In real sense—fifty-seven-year-long career marathon. Some people have not even lived that long, leave alone working, and are resting six feet underground. Surely, the Almighty God has been really kind to me! Now retired, I have no earthly boss, no schedule, and no worries.

I am answerable only to my creator—the Almighty God to whom be honor, glory, and majesty. Amen!

Now I sleep whenever I feel like, rise up whenever, eat whenever, go wherever, do whatever, talk to whomever about whatever for whatever length of time. Admittedly, I feel totally liberated, independent, and free at last!

Voluntary Role

Since my early childhood, I have enjoyed helping other people from all walks of life by caring and sharing my blessings with whoever is my neighbor. I pledge to engage in this role so long as God keeps me alive; keeps me sound physically, mentally, and spiritually. I confess that I am really intrigued and influenced by the glaring aspects of servanthood of Joshua and Caleb in the Bible. These brothers served God faithfully and selflessly. Having been created equal with other human beings on the planet, the spirit of God has revealed to me that I am compassionate, empathetic, generous, humble, kind, loving, merciful, passionate, patient, sensitive, and understanding.

Having been born and raised in a village under very challenging economic and social circumstances, I can easily identify with the struggles that the have-nots and have nothing at all go through in real-life situations. I am thrilled by a sense of belonging, originality, identity, and a sense of purpose (BIOP). God's Spirit within me cautions me—we should not be saying no to things we can say yes to. I trust God is able to deliver in His own terms those who are passionate to do well—until good becomes better and better best! There is nothing much else to do to what is at its "best."

Caution: Do not allow anyone or anything to discourage you from following up on your lifetime dream. Just do it, and do it right—it is your absolute right!

Amazingly, my heart continually beats for the poor in material things (impoverished), the illiterate, the lonely, the elderly, the handicapped, the sick, the low in spirit, and the hopeless. Guided by God's Spirit and heart conviction, I founded "Village Food Bank Foundation" (VFBF, Inc.), a nonprofit organization. The mission and vision are to solely care for the needs and the well-being of the populations identified above, simply, "bringing hope and smiles to the hopeless." VFBF wishes to be simply recognized as a "channel of encouragement and help" to the helpless. Please join me in this endeavor.

Gratitude

The writer wishes to recognize the entire Ngaines family members for their hospitality, generosity, and the universal roles of opening their homes both in the United States and Kenya and catering for the destitute, friendless, handicapped, helpless, homeless, hopeless, hungry, jobless, lonely, lost, neighbors, poor, sick, strangers, travelers, and visitors—just to name a few.

The Outlook

Net proceeds from sales and distribution of this publication will be designated to benefit the following charities:

1. Village Food Bank Foundation, Inc. (VFBF)

The fund will enable funding of programs and projects that would benefit the general public. VFBF is a public charity "helping others help themselves" by working and supporting themselves and their families with the ultimate goal of "self-sufficiency and self-esteem."

2. Late Jennifer W. Ngaine Memorial Fund.

The funds will provide financial support to individuals and families in need of medical attention for heart disorders. Jennifer died naturally at age forty-one due to "congenital abnormal origin of coronary arteries."

3. Fund treatment and research on dementia, pancreatic, and prostate cancer epidemics on village adults.

Lifetime Achievements/ Accomplishments

- Got a burning charcoal tattoo on my left shoulder at age eight.

- Had my first ten cents Kenyan currency money gift at age six as a Christmas gift from an uncle.

- Incidentally became head of my household at age twelve following the detention of Dad, Mom, and older sister during the Mau Mau uprising in Kenya in 1954.

- Went through tribal custom/ritual circumcision in the village at age twelve.

- Planted own one hundred coffee cash plants at age thirteen.

- Built my first one-bedroom mud house (sixteen feet by twelve feet) at age fifteen.

- Attended a day middle school *six* miles away from home or a twelve-mile journey (R/T) five days a week.

- Received my first academic award in fifth grade by solving a puzzle involving a father who had three boys, two baseball caps, and wanted the boys to wear the caps evenly over a thirty-day period.

- Accepted Jesus Christ as my Lord and Savior at age twelve.

- Named "head prefect" (captain) to a 150-student body at age seventeen.

- Bought first pair of shoes at age eighteen.

- Passed a one-week job interview in 1960 attended by one thousand candidates. Was among the top ten out of 250 successful candidates and served the organization (ERH) for eleven years.

- Got married in a Christian church ceremony at age twenty-four in 1966. Still married to my sweetheart.

- Resigned from my first job after eleven-year service to pursue higher education. Received no retirement benefits.

- Flew into the United States for further studies in 1971 with only $10 as pocket money.

- Enrolled in college at age thirty with three children on the side.

- Educated myself through a two-year and four-year colleges without financial help while working full-time and supporting a family of eight (wife and three children, my parents, and my two youngest siblings).

- Educated my sister and brother through high school and vocational schools.

- Achieved an associate degree at age thirty-two, a bachelor's degree at thirty-six, and a master's degree at thirty-nine.

- Was the first member in my family to earn a college degree.

- Had our lastborn at age thirty-seven while still in college.

- Raised four children and put them through college.

- Became a driver—first-time—in 1973 at age thirty-one.

- Owned my first car (a used Buick special, gift from a friend) in 1973.

- Owned our first home in US in 1988.

- Earned a certified public accountant (CPA) certification in 1993 at age fifty-one, recognized globally.

- Earned a chartered global management accountant (CGMA) certification at age seventy-one, recognized globally.

- Obtained a US alien status green card after seventeen years of residency and citizenship six years later.

- Obtained the US citizenship in 1993—the greatest country in the world that guarantees liberty, freedom, and independence through self-representation (self-appointed attorney).

- Served the Federal Government as an accountant/auditor/programs inspector for fifteen years.

- Served as the first African ruling elder (RE) in a Presbyterian church of four-hundred-plus members for over thirty years.

- Have no criminal record.

- Have no known enemies.

- Have innumerable friends—Jesus Christ is my best friend.

- Love God, and God loves me—love every good thing!

- Improved quality of economic, social, and spiritual life for all members of my immediate and extended family members.

- Improved international social skills and professional recognition through written professional examinations.

- Founded Village Food Bank Foundation, Inc. in 2016 while still on full-time employment. The foundation is supporting over two hundred needy families monthly in Maryland and my home village, Kiangua, Kenya.

- Retired at age seventy-five in January 2018 with full benefits.

Hobbies and Personal Traits

1. Accountant

2. Analyst

3. Auditor

4. Chef

5. Christian

6. Communicator

7. Consultant

8. Counselor

9. Disciple

10. Discussant

11. Director

12. Educator

13. Elder

14. Entertainer

15. Entrepreneur

16. Extrovert

17. Farmer

18. Father

19. Grandparent

20. Historian

21. Husband

22. Investigator

23. Leader

24. Manager

25. MC

26. Mediator

27. Mentor

28. Motivator

29. Orator

30. Parent

31. Planner

32. Pragmatist

33. Preacher

34. Reader/writer

35. Researcher

36. Speaker

37. Teacher

38. Traveler

Humorous Notes

1. *One-Mile Walk*

According to Mom's account, she had taken me and my older sister to a seasonal community festivity. The festivity featured food, drinks, and local dancing. All this time, Mom carried me on her back so I could see the display of events over her shoulders. I have no idea what age I was, but evidently, I hadn't been around that much—I would guess a little over two years. My older sister was on her feet. At some point, the local dancing became so interesting, and according to my mom, I danced wildly on her back, making me unbearable and a total discomfort to her. Mom put me down, found a way to the front row, where, according to her, I danced nonstop.

When the event ended and it was time to return home, I attempted to reclaim my ride on Mom's back. She utterly blocked me. Pathetically, I was compelled to walk—crying for a mile.

Coincidentally, I graduated with honors and never rode on anybody's back since. Admittedly, I loved dancing ever since the early introductory course. Thanks, Mom.

2. *Accidental Fall off a Tree*

I believe I was aged between seven and eight years on one breezy July afternoon. It had rained in the morning, but the weather had cleared up quite a bit. I was assigned to watch over a flock of goats and sheep just a stone's throw from our homestead. I had frequently watched monkeys in bushes nearby climb trees and hop from one branch of a tree to another. Honestly, I'm a good imitator of things, and like monkeys, I had practiced and climbed on and off trees for a while without an incident. On this particular afternoon, I got bored just watching the animals and idling. Unfortunately, things turned out hazardously. I climbed the target tree all the way to the top without an incident. While descending, almost halfway through, I stepped on a branch that didn't quite support my weight. The tree was wet. Helplessly, I slipped, fell off, and landed on some green shrubs below.

Unfortunately, the shrubs had covered a sharp stem of a young tree that was cut off earlier. The stem had dried off and had hardened.

The fatal stem went through my left thigh and chopped off a chunk of thigh muscles. I bled profusely and passed out. The flock had found their way home without me at sunset, but Rachi was no-show. My father thought that was weird and started calling out my name loudly. When I didn't respond, a search ensued, and in my peril, I was discovered unconscious under the shrubs. The nearest hospital was five miles away, and it was already dark. Also, no local transportation was available, so I wasn't rushed to the hospital. Some nourishment might have kept me alive overnight.

I had no recollections of what transpired after the fall. The next morning, I found myself on a stretcher and on the shoulders of my father and my uncle on my father's side. I knew I was on my way to the hospital because the couple talked about it and other nasty things about me. I said nothing. I felt a terrible nagging pain on my left thigh, but I told myself not to scream or yell. The entire left leg was swollen. I simply groaned silently. When I raised my head and peeped through, I noticed my thigh was covered with tree bucking and fastened with sisal ropes (this was the ancient way of stopping or slowing bleeding on a fresh cut). Well, we got to the hospital, and I got admitted. While the hospital staff was still cleaning and preparing me, the two gentlemen that brought me to the hospital had departed. They had to walk back home five miles and, of course, the day was already well spent. I never saw either one until I was discharged and returned home alone about three weeks later. The hospital had provided the meals, so nothing came from home. Sadly, I don't recall anyone visiting me during the ordeal. I kept the bandage on the healed thigh until the muscles relaxed and reconditioned. My father's final warning to me was, "If you have any further incidents with trees or any childish, foolish, reckless, and senseless accidents and incidents—you are on your own!" You know, I would say there were incidents—but they were minor in nature. The resultant scar, though, is a remarkable landmark in my body, and finally, I do admit that I hopped into things (rides, etc.), but I completely stayed clear of climbing things.

3. *Rachi's First Shoe*

Until December 1959, I had never owned, worn a shoe, or known the size of my feet. I had walked barefoot all my life. At this particular time, I was on my way to my first job interview. That morning, I had walked eight miles, barefoot, on a dusty road to a shopping center on a major road. I had to catch a country bus to another town, spend the night, then catch another country bus to a town near a railway station and then catch a train to the interview venue. The storekeeper at the shopping center had shoes but had to first measure by feet to determine the size. A brown shoe that looked good was the closest but wasn't quite my size. The shopkeeper suggested that if I washed my feet and slipped into the shoes while still wet and soapy, they'd fit just fine. I cooperated, and it worked.

Shortly, the country bus showed up, and I hopped in for a fourhour ride. On arrival at the next stopover, I couldn't walk. My feet had swollen, were numb, and stuck in the shoes. A sympathizer suggested that I seek help from a shoe repairer nearby. When I did, the repairman recommended we slice the shoes on the edges so that air could get in and allow the feet to breathe.

He warned that if I took the shoe off, the feet might not get back in. I concurred and wisely slept with the shoes on all night and the next day.

Two days later, I arrived at the interview site. Immediately, I borrowed a knife and converted the shoes into open-end sandals.

The move worked. By God's grace, I got hired and spent my first salary to buy me a proper-size shoe. If your shoe size is ten and a half, you know what I am talking about. I have worn a proper-size shoe ever since.

4. *A Street Holdup*

My roommate was walking home from work around midnight back in 1972. We lived in a semi-bad neighborhood that one never knew what goes on at night until something happens. Three blocks away from where we lived, a stranger stopped him and demanded money. My roommate replied that all he had was $5. The intruder asked my roommate whether he was new in town. My roommate replied yes and also that he was from Africa and was attending college.

The holdup man asked him which country he was from, and he answered Kenya.

The holdup man screamed, "Jomo Kenyatta's country! That's my kind of man. Listen, you can easily get killed if you continue to walk the streets at night, well dressed, without money on you. Keep the $5 and give to the guy in the next block. He takes no bullshit." My roommate did not understand what bullshit meant.

5. *Outing to a First Movie Theatre*

A colleague and a friend that I had met in Nairobi following my first job invited me to a movie on a weekend. This was in 1960, and Kenya was still under the colonial rule. Accordingly, the Great Britain's anthem, with the Union Jack flying, had to be played prior to the start of all public events. The theater seats were designed to fold and allow the attendees to stand up during the playing of the anthem. To sit down, the guests were required to manually push the seats down. This being my first time exposure, I didn't have a clue about this process, and my friend probably assumed I knew what to do. Incidentally, I sat on the upper edge of the seat until the intermission.

Even though I was the tallest figure in the auditorium while seated, it didn't bother me. I was steadily focused on the movie feature on the screen like everybody else. After the break, my friend refreshed and taught me the trick. It has always been refreshing to share the occurrence.

6. *A Lottery Win*

During the early 1970s, gambling was illegal in the state of Maryland. Somehow, number gambling (today's lottery) was going on in Maryland behind the scenes. I lived and worked in the District of Columbia. On this day, January 2, 1973, I illegally gambled $2 straight on number 733 out of the blue. The number was allotted to me in a service waiting sequence somewhere in prior weeks.

Unexpectedly, the number man called me at one o'clock that same morning and excitedly announced, "Your number hit." Except in literal sense, I had never witnessed the word *hit* being used to express a win. We did not understand one another, so we agreed to meet later that afternoon. Sure enough, at 1:00 p.m. at an agreed location, the number man handed me $1,050. I gave him a $50 tip, and my friends thought I was a "good-luck charm." A year later, on the same date, I gambled number 722 $1 straight. I had picked the numbers from my first car registration—Washington DC plate numbers. I won $530 and tipped $30.

When gambling was legalized in both DC and MD, I played occasionally for a while. When I realized no wins, I decided to abandon the habit. Prolonged gambling to me could be addictive and might lead to debts. By sheer luck, I incidentally picked up $35 on separate occasions—$5 off the street after packing my car, $10 in an empty packing space, and a $20 bill that popped up when a double-door swung open in a public building. Since nobody around made a claim, I kept it.

7. *Warning—Don't Walk!*

A Kenyan visitor in downtown DC attempted to run across an intersection while the sign Don't Walk was on. At the other side of the street, a police officer was waiting and announced to the visitor

that he was going to issue him a "jaywalking" citation. The visitor queried what that meant, and the officer explained. The visitor responded to the officer that he saw the sign all right but interpreted it to mean run, and so he ran. The officer thought that was funny and asked the visitor whether he was new in town. When the visitor answered yes, the officer advised the visitor to be more alert when crossing intersections.

8. *Do You Have a Kool?*

"Kool" to me sounded like "cool" under a weather situation.

A stranger stopped me on a DC street back in the years during the daytime and asked me if I had a Kool. I thought since it was a nice and cool day, he was being social, wanted to discuss the weather, and I naturally answered, "Yes."

He asked me to give him one, and I asked him what he meant. He repeated, "A Kool."

Well, I got confused. When he realized that I wasn't getting it, he inquired whether I was new in town, and I said yes. He discharged me with a cold, "Take care!"

I thought that was a threat, and I took off in a hurry. Later, I realized that Kool was a cigarette.

9. *Fighting Fire under the Hood of a Car?*

My first car in America was a used four-door Buick Special 1963. A retired elderly friend in a building I worked at as a desk clerk had given it to me as a Christmas gift. It had a nice body, but the engine was not healthy. At one time, it stalled and failed to start.

I guess I might have flooded the carburetor by overcranking it. I had the hood up when suddenly the fire engulfed from the engine.

The only thing I had on hand was a soggy oily towel. Frantically, as I was fighting the fire with my towel tool, a total stranger saw what was going, had stopped his car on the street, ran to where I was, and extinguished the fire instantly. It appeared he had the extinguisher in his car.

He looked at me straight in the eye and exclaimed, "You are as damn as shit. You could have put your ass on fire!" and walked away.

That's the first time I witnessed a portable fire extinguisher—not to mention that this was the sloppiest firefighting encounter ever.

10. *Shocking Professional Advice*

In good faith and mutual respect, I had decided to seek professional advice from one of my Jewish professors. I had enrolled for an auditing course that this particular professor taught during my senior year. My progressive performance and evaluations in his class were good. I noted that the enrollment for the class was low, but I did not have any concerns. Incidentally, a fellow student that was taking the same course noticed me in the cafeteria during a lunch break and joined me. Unsolicited, he shared that our professor was a racist and disliked minorities. My classmate further shared that he was repeating this same course and blamed the professor for failing him discriminately. That was strange and hard for me to comprehend and did deter my desire to seek the professor's advice.

When the opportunity permitted, I and the professor talked all right. However, expecting some encouragement and what have you, he advised me not to waste time studying for CPA exams. He reasoned that it took years to prepare, review courses were pricey, and that minorities and foreigners had a slim chance of passing the exam, leave alone finding jobs. I passed his course with a B grade.

Later, I privately learned that B's were the top grades in his classes—he did not believe A grades were realistic. Fifteen (15) years later, I had earned a CPA credential and had a good job too. I hurried back to my alma mater to surprise my former auditing professor. Sadly, I got word that he had become mentally disoriented and was forced to retire on the grounds of public interests. Well, I "walk by faith and not by sight."

11. *Microsoft Word Nightmare—Did You Save?*

This was a fateful day in my professional career! I had just entered into a joint agreement with one of my associate public accounting firms—Allmond & Company, CPAs, to review and prepare the annual report on the operations of a savings and loans organization in the state of Virginia. During the week, about lunch time, there came an announcement that the group would meet in a restaurant nearby and have lunch together. Also, a reminder was added that the group would be exchanging notes relative to the progress of the project. No problem up to this point.

The associates took turns to share their respective updates.

When it was my turn, I did fine with the presentation of the updates until the lead partner inquired, "Rachi, did you save your work when you signed off for lunch?"

I hurriedly answered in the affirmative, but guess what? I did not save my work, and ironically, I had lost everything! Microsoft had just introduced the *first version* of the *Word documents, and the orientation process took a while. Today, saving is automatic with the latest edition of Windows.* Momentarily, a chill went through my brain, and I sweated quite a bit. Realizing my dilemma, I curtailed my lunchbreak and rushed back to work. During lunch, the associates were reminded that a written summary of updates was needed early the next day for briefing of the principals. To catch up and recapture the lost effort, Rachi stayed behind at the work site for an additional five hours of *unpaid* time. Note: there were no laptops as yet. I learned a lesson. From then on I have been saving a Word document every fifteen minutes or sooner. Unsaved document is tantamount to *sudden death*. Imagine Jesus returning to earth and you are not saved—you are dead alive (i.e., if you had planned to go to heaven)!

12. *First Microwave-Use Disaster*

I am bad news when it comes to experiments: First timer here and there. Well, remember the phrase, "We learn from mistakes, or the school of hard knocks." I had an opportunity to use a microwave for the first time in my life.

I had bought a cold sandwich snack for a quick lunch from a nearby 7-Eleven store in the building where I worked. I had earlier noticed people walking to this little machine that I had never seen and knew nothing about. American folks like sharing information, so one of the microwave users briefly explained the operating procedures to me. When I returned from the 7-Eleven, I noticed the machine was available, and I took the opportunity to warm my snack. Equipped with the operating instructions learned from my volunteer instructor earlier on, I properly placed the sandwich at the center of the plate, closed the door, selected five minutes from the dial, and pressed Start.

As I watched through the glass door, the sandwich became smaller, smaller, smaller, and even smaller. I didn't know how to turn the machine off.

Passersby and onlookers could not figure out what in the world I was warming up. Finally, when the machine stopped and I opened the door, the finished product was a tiny well-baked and hard-baked cashew nut. None of the onlookers spoke, nor did I. I had this weird imagination that it might swell back on after cooling down, but it didn't. That was my surprise lunch for the day. I just fasted for the day.

13. *Waiting for a Bus on Wrong Side of Street*

For years in Kenya, I was used to keeping on the left side of the street based on the British system that had been established in the country for years. In the United States, it's just the opposite—you keep to the right. Cousin George and others had coached me adequately on these basics. Based on the instincts, though, I was still programmed to keeping left on the street. All I knew was the bus number that I needed to board with the sign showing the destination.

The buses had the numbers, but destinations were not clearly identifiable based on my limited knowledge at that time.

Funny enough, I must have waited for a whole hour before realizing that I was on the wrong side of the street.

Quickly I corrected myself, crossed the street, and in no time, the right-number bus with a familiar destination showed up.

Soon, I was on my way and never again forgot what side of the street I needed to be on while in America.

14. *School Attendance on a Public Holiday*

Besides the wrong-side-of-the-street incident, it took me a whole year to familiarize myself with American holidays, events, and seasons. Lots of foreigners, even today, have no clear conscience regarding seasonal timings and which holiday represents what.

Mine was a Columbus Day (October) in the District of Columbia in 1972. On this day, I showed up at school right on time for my scheduled class—so I thought. As I attempted to enter the building, the security guard demanded to know why I was there. I replied I was there for a class that was about to start. Apparently, he got puzzled and asked me whether I was aware it was a "Columbus Day" holiday. "No!" I answered. Incidentally, the security guard was substitute instructor for that day. Sometimes, we learn the hard way—don't we? When is Fall Backwards, Parents', St. Patrick's, Trick or Treat, and Valentine's Days?

15. *A New Arrival in US Dressed in Three-Piece Suit in Summer*

A new student from Kenya arrived in the US during summer. It was in July. He wasn't sure where he was going to reside, so he stopped by the Kenyan embassy in DC to seek further advice. Since it was hot, the vehicle he rode from the airport had air conditioning.

At the embassy, he exited the vehicle, paid the fare, and claimed his luggage. The air temperatures were in the nineties. Momentarily, he started sweating profusely but didn't know why. In Kenya, July is chilly. As a precaution, he had on a three-piece suit and a turtleneck sweater, just to be on the safe side. Someone at the embassy suggested he take off the upper two piece of the suit and leave the sweater on. He continued to sweat. Right then he remembered he had some shirts in the suitcase. Another misfortune—he could not find the key to the luggage right away.

Quick solution: Broke the lock and accessed a change of clothing.

The rest is history.

16. *Two Cousins Lost at the Airport for Three Days*

Two cousins had accompanied each other on a flight from Nairobi, Kenya, to Dulles International Airport in Virginia. They were to attend Coppin State College in Baltimore, Maryland. Their uncle, who was a professor in that college, had made arrangements to pick them up upon arrival. So far, everybody was on time. Somehow, something went bizarre. The uncle reported to the arrival area of the international flights, noticed that the flight had landed, and waited for a while. Finally, when all passengers had exited and the uncle realized that his guests did not appear, he resolved to have their names announced over the intercom just after a short waiting period. The effort was fruitless, so he went home. Little did he know that one of the nephews had a minor issue with the US Immigration. By the time he got cleared to enter the US, the uncle had left the airport, and neither one knew what was happening.

It took them three days to reconnect with the uncle (Friday through Sunday). At the airport, the cousins lived on donuts until the airport security noticed their dilemma. When approached, they quickly narrated the miscommunication including sharing the uncle's home phone number with the security. When asked why they failed to call their uncle during the interim, they replied that they didn't know how to make a call and were afraid to ask for fear of being arrested. Sympathetically, the airport security called the uncle for them.

When the uncle learned that the nephews were lost at the airport for three days, he became furious. He rushed to the airport the second time and picked them up. Still in fury, he did not greet them or talk to them over a fifty-mile journey. It took a while for the duo to normalize relationships. Truly, beginnings are tough, but some endings are smooth. I understand that the two cousins are still in America and eventually became US citizens.

17. *A Student to US Denied Entry due to Self-Incriminating Information in the Letter of Invitation*

During an interrogation of a new Kenyan student at an entry point in the East Coast of the United States, the following dialogue ensued:

Immigration Officer. At what address in America will you be residing?

Student Visitor. I do not remember. But my cousin is here at the airport to pick me up.

Immigration Officer. Do you have your cousin's telephone number?

Student Visitor. I do not remember. Like I said, he is already here to pick me up.

Immigration Officer. Do you have a letter with a return address from your cousin?

Student Visitor. Oh yes!

Result: When the officer read the contents of the letter, it revealed the worst case scenario—there was a paragraph advising the student to arrive early in summer so he could hustle and raise some pocket money prior to starting school in the fall. Instantaneously, he was asked to step aside, detained, and forced to take the next flight back home. He called his cousin from back home a week later to explain the nasty ending.

18. *A Lucky Escape!*

An Exchange Program Guest at a US entry point agrees in good faith that she would accept a job offer and still allowed entry. The interchange went as follows:

Immigration Officer. Would you accept a job offer in the United States while on the exchange program status?

Guest. Yes! That is remarkable kindness on part of the host. It would be rude of me as a guest to refuse such a generous offer!

Immigration Officer. Great...and welcome to America! Lucky, lucky escape!

19. *It Is Only a Chicken*

A Kenyan fella who worked nightshifts (12:00–8.00 a.m.) was preparing a chicken dinner when he decided to briefly nap on the couch while a whole chicken was cooking in the oven at 370 degrees temperature.

The next thing he witnessed was a squad of firefighters inside his apartment with water hoses, shouting, "Get out! Get out!" That's when he realized there was a lot of smoke coming out of the oven.

He yelled back, "It's only a chicken!" The chicken had overcooked in the oven.

Fire squad said, "Get out! Get out!"

Well, he did. However, by the time the squad calmed down the smoke, the chicken dinner was a total mess.

He later learned that the next-door neighbor noticed the flavored smoke, got scared that someone was roasting inside, and dialed 911.

20. *A Village Doctor*

A village in Kenya had welcomed back one of their favorite sons that had travelled to USA for further studies and returned home after eight (8) years with a Doctor of Philosophy degree (PhD) in political science. Ironically, the doctorate title to the village folks was construed to mean a medical doctor. Accordingly, throngs of people infected with wounds, diseases, and health disorders waited at his village home to be seen and treated.

When it became clear he was not the kind of a doctor the crowd had anticipated, the would-be patients suddenly became antagonists and wondered, "Why did he waste all that money and time overseas to study nothing?" It was a shock both ways. Later on, the Early next morning, the sixth grader was the first one up. He ate some cereal/breakfast and ran by the parents' room for goodbyes. He knocked on the door, but when no one opened, he noticed the door was unlocked. He peeped through and observed that only Mom was in bed and looked *terrible and messy*. Next, he went by nanny's room and noticed through her partially covered window that is where his dad was and was *on top of the nanny*.

Quickly, he ran by his brother's room and realized it *stunk*— because nobody had changed his diapers for hours.

Anyway, as always, he took his bus to school.

By chance, he was the last one in his class to make the presentation on the assignment.

The sixth grader stated, "Sir, the economy looks terrible and messy because the capital is screwing labor, and the future stinks."

The instructor underlined that the report was effectively precise, and audience concurred. Well, with precision in mind, I earned the CPA certification through five-part handwritten exams three year later (1993).

21. *The Resounding Ahah . . . Ahah . . . Ahah! Dentist*

I had never been to a dentist's office all my life until this time. I must have been a resident in the US for two good years when suddenly I could not tolerate any warm or cold drink in my mouth.

Without much choice, I was compelled to visit a nearby dentist. Soon after the examination started, the dentist was exclaiming, "Ahah…Ahah…Ahah!"

When I inquired what it was, he answered, "Cavities!"

I had never heard of the word before, so he explained. Again, I hadn't been to a dentist's office ever since. I am talking about over forty-five years. Seemingly, I needed annual checkups, fillings, and cleaning. I got hooked up, and sadly, this is one of my costliest bills every year.

Out of ignorance and easy access to sweets in America, I had fallen in love with candies, cookies, cakes, and sweets. In Kenya, I grew up without the benefit of tasting these goodies, you know. You whole Kenya was shocked to learn that the PhD credential the village had condemned was the first such academic title in Africa, Kenya included. He actually became successful in his political career.

22. *Precision at Best!*

Based on advice by a trusted colleague in 1990, I enrolled in a private CPA review course in preparation for sitting for the CPA exam in the spring of that year. In his introductory remarks, the course instructor reiterated that precision in answering essay questions was imperative and gave a narrative example. He recited that a sixth grader in a family, probably a boy, had come home with a homework assignment of which he had no foreknowledge and was discouraged. The teacher had warned everyone in class to be ready to share their answers at the beginning of class the next day. When the father asked what the assignment was, the son stated that it was about economics. The boy added that the teacher needs explanation as to what it is, how it affects the future, and personal thoughts.

The father responded by stating, "This is easy, son…listen!" He went on to explain that economics is built around components or factors like (a) capital, (b) economy, (c) labor, and (d) the future.

He likened himself to capital, his wife to the economy, the nanny to labor, and the sixth grader and his baby brother to the future. He concluded by describing to the son that Dad, as the capital, makes the money which he gives to your mom, who is the economy for this family. Mom hires the nanny, the labor, who gives help around the house. Mom buys groceries, clothes, and pays other family bills. We're doing this so that you and your brother could have a great future.

The boy acknowledged excitedly by saying, "Wow! Dad, that was great! I got it!"

have read my life story in the good old days, so you know where I am coming from. In the West, I almost had candies for dinner until I learned from my hard lesson from the Ahah! Dentist. It's been costly!

Advice: Just taste candies—just don't eat them.

23. *Rescue from a Snowstorm*

In the winter of 1981, I and a Kenyan neighbor in Maryland planned a trip to a country market seventy miles away from residence. I was the designated driver. We made the trip to the market with ease and made the shopping lists. A select number of families had included their selections, and we made good on that too. We had planned the trip without any regard for the possible change of weather. Instead of radio music or news, we had our best home music sounds throughout the outward journey. Surprise, surprise, surprise.

Soon after we started the return trip, snow started falling. Twenty miles later, it became a snowstorm, and we couldn't see the roadway. At this point, we turned on the radio and didn't like what we heard. The announcements were intentional and repetitive: "Warning!

If you are on the road, pull over and wait for help!" then added, "All roads in Maryland are closed. Snowplowing is suspended till further notice...just wait for rescue in your car and please, please...don't drive." Well, we heeded to the warnings, got rescued within hours, and camped into an elementary school dining hall nearby until the next day.

24. *Rachi . . . Are You Gay?*

I had received my first weekly payroll check in 1972 that I needed to cash. It was on a Friday. My employer's bank was a few blocks up the street, so I just walked over and presented the check to the bank teller. The teller demanded a picture ID, but I had none.

The teller asked me whether I knew anyone in the bank that could be my witness so I could cash the check, but my answer was no. At that point, my check was returned to me, and while on my way out, I ran into someone I knew. He was on the same mission as mine—that is, to cash a check.

When he realized my dilemma, he volunteered to assist me. We returned to the same teller that had turned me away a few minutes earlier. My friend explained that he was willing to be my witness and presented his credentials that were never questioned. I cashed the check because I had no bank account at the time. I waited for my friend to finish, and we walked out together.

We continued to talk in a real jovial mood. As we exited the bank, a colleague of mine at work was about to enter the bank, and I attempted to introduce him to my friend. Almost instantaneously their facial expressions changed in a downcast way. Apparently, they knew one another. The following Monday, my workmate didn't hesitate to approach me with a very direct question: "Rachi, are you gay?" to which I answered, "Yes!" He instantly reacted by shouting,

"Rachi is gay! Rachi is gay!" The bystanders were astonished.

You see, I was primarily educated under the British system, and the *gay* word that I knew and was reaffirming was described by *Oxford Dictionary* (English) as "happily excited; high in spirit; bright, lively, and brilliant." The American *Webster Dictionary* defines *gay* as "a homosexual male." I had to defend myself profusely.

The backbone of the episode was illuminated by the fact that the friend that had assisted me to cash the payroll check at the bank was openly known by those around to be gay per the Webster. He worked in the area and lived in DC. As a new guy in the block, probably I was the only one that didn't know homosexuality was a lifestyle, and that Garry, my friend, was gay. Unfortunately, my workmate had misinterpreted my warm interaction with Garry as relational instead of social, of course. Guess what, though—since then I have learned to distinguish the characteristics between the body languages of the heterosexuals as opposed to those of homosexuals. I dare say that I am openly and naturally heterosexual (straight). We have come a long way—and still have a long way to go, don't we? Seriously, the world changes from one area to the next.

Worthwhile Notes

During my active life on earth for almost 80 years, I have observed and witnessed that in general, life is personal and unique and none of it is identical even among the "identical twins". From a common perspective, I have experienced that the following facts in no special order, form a "Universal Life-Pattern."

A)

- The most destructive element in life is .... **Worry**
- The greatest joy in life is.. **Giving**
- The greatest personal loss is............................ <u>Self</u> **respect**
- The most satisfying work is............................ **Helping Others**
- The ugliest personality trait is .... **Selfishness**
- The greatest shot in the arm is ....**Encouragement**
- The worst human display is..................................... **Pride**
- The greatest personal problem to overcome is......................... **Fear**
- The most effective sleeping pill is .... **Peace of Mind**
- The most crippling personal weakness is .... **Excuses**
- The most powerful force in life is............................ **Love**
- The most poisonous act in life is .... **Gossip**
- The world's most incredible computer is the............ **Human Brain**
- The most powerful personal force is............................ **Willpower**
- The lowest position in life is...................... **Hopelessness**
- The most dangerous act is...................... Gossip
- The two most re-assuring words are .... **"I Can"**
- The most worthless life emotion is .... **Self-pity**
- The most prized personal trait is .... **Integrity.**
- The most contagious spirit is...................... **Enthusiasm.**
- The greatest asset in life is...................... **Faith**
- The deadliest human weapon is .... **The Tongue**
- The well-prized personal appeal is...................... **A Smile**

- o The most powerful means of communing with God is .... **Prayer**
- o The best kept secret is between believer and............................ **God**
- o The top secrets and kept by.. **God**
- o The most precious friend for Christians is............................ **Jesus**
- o Th most unselfish gift is... **Volunteering**
- o The best relationship on earth is.................................. **Friendship**
- o The cruelest human antagonist is.. **Death**
- o The worst human adversary is... **Satan**

Reader; Feel free to add your own convictions . . .

B) Mixed Facts-of-life:

- Ascending is harder comparted to descending
- Believers are the most powerful community on earth
- Broken hearts are crippled
- Cheats and lies are first cousins
- Easy to be born and easy to die . . . you are born . . . you live . . . you die!
- God reinstalls broken hearts
- Hard to stay alive healthy and doing well
- Hard to find something you really like/love
- Hard to find a safe place to live
- Hard to find a true and trustworthy friend
- Hard to find undisputed truth
- Re-union does not guarantee unity
- Pretenders are worse than murderers
- There's nothing easy in life
- No one questions the truth
- Parents' divorces torture their children
- The color of the skin is secondary to ones' character
- The environment does not determine destiny
- There are no two-party secrets
- The rich and famous are not necessarily . . . the healthiest
- There is no working hard without being productive
- Undeveloped ideas die a natural death

Note: If I add what others have experienced we would be here indefinitely.

C) Personal Special observations . . .
- o Love is **BLIND**
- o Love ends when you stop **CARING**
- o Love is the strongest **FOUNDATION** on earth
- o Hope ends when you stop **BELIEVING** and start **DOUBTING**
- o Life ends when you become desperate and stop **DREAMING**
- o You do not **FINISH** what you do not **START**
- o What we see is the **PRODUCT** of what has been **PLANNTED**
- o You are not Just **ANYBODY**—you're **SOMEBODY!**
- o God created each of us uniquely . . . you're **UNIQUE**
- o Staying **BUSY OR OCCUPIED** does not prove **PRODUCTIVITY and of course,**
- o Yesterday is **HISTOTY, today is a GIFT** and tomorrow is **MYSTERY.**

D) The less and less of Century 21
- • Attitude is care<u>less</u>
- • Babies are father<u>less</u>
- • Break-ups are count<u>less</u>
- • Cars are key<u>less</u>
- • Children are mother<u>less</u>
- • Cooking is fire<u>less</u>
- • Covid-19 pandemic has made commercial buildings and businesses use<u>less</u>
- • Covid-19 virus couldn't care<u>less</u>; has caused billions of job<u>less</u>ness
- • Crime rate is sense<u>less</u>
- • Divorces are count<u>less</u>
- • Dresses are sleeve<u>less</u>
- • Everything is becoming less and <u>less</u>
- • Feelings are heart<u>less</u>
- • Foods are fat<u>less</u>
- • Hopes are end<u>less</u>
- • Ignorance of the truth is thought<u>less</u>

- Job security is becoming less and <u>less</u>
- Leaders are shame<u>less</u>
- Lies are value<u>less</u>
- Morality is becoming less and <u>less</u>
- Most humans have become speech<u>less</u>
- Most people couldn't care <u>less</u>
- Most market stocks are worth<u>less</u>
- Relationships are meaning<u>less</u>
- Self-injury is pain<u>less</u>
- Taking good advice is cost<u>less</u>
- Tires are tube<u>less</u>
- Too much of anything is <u>useless</u>
- Wealth has become meaning<u>less</u>
- Wearing a car seatbelt is effort<u>less</u>
- Women are fear<u>less</u>
- Youths at-large are job<u>less</u>

Reader; Make your own list in your next story un<u>less</u> you want to remain help<u>less</u> . . .

References

1. Wangari, Esther. *Ameru (Heritage Library of African Peoples East Africa)*

2. *The Holy Bible (NIV)*

3. Gathigira, Stanley. *Miikarire Ya Agikuyu*

4. Kenyatta, Jomo. *Facing Mount Kenya*

5. Elkins, Caroline. *The Mau Mau*

6. The Gideons International. *365 Readings through the Bible*

7. Daily Bread Devotions from "Daily Bread Ministries"

8. Hearsay and interrogations

9. Inquiries, interviews, and dialogues

10. Extensive literary readings

11. Hundreds of literary materials; volumes of textbooks, periodicals, professional journals, magazines, case studies, research materials, real-life experiences, and witnessing. Direct questions, direct answers

About the Author

Rachi Ngaine was born and raised in an African Kenyan village. His parents were unschooled but were God loving. He is the second-born in a pile of six siblings. He grew up typically in a traditional rural village and close family ties—under very challenging economic and social circumstances. Rachi is blessed with unique character, goals, and roots. He started real life by performing small tasks around the homestead and gradually assumed larger roles of shepherding family goats/sheep and volunteering as a foot messenger (mailman) for neighbors in his village. Rachi met Christ while a teenager, was born again (transformed) and continues to walk by faith.

He is a survivor of a fierce civil war, Mau Mau uprise against the colonial dominance in Kenya in the early fifties. At age twelve, Rachi was compelled to suddenly take on the role of head of the household for his family due to an abrupt arrest and imprisonment of his three senior members of the family (both parents and the older sister).

Without proof, the seniors were accused of participating in outlawed oathtaking and supporting an illegal clandestine movement. The aftermath of the war led to losses of life for tens of close relatives on both sides of the family including properties. After attaining minimum cutting age, Rachi voluntarily and courageously underwent a traditional village circumcision to achieve tribal adulthood status.

Due to economic conditions, he started elementary school late.

However, he completed public schooling and obtained a clerical job with a regional organization and served for eleven years. While working in Kenya, Rachi got married to his one-and-only wife fifty-three years ago. Their marriage produced four children of which three are alive and well. From the earliest days, Rachi had developed a unique appetite for good education and a solid career path in a tough economic environment.

In pursuance of his academic dreams and greener pastures, he applied and got admission to study accounting, business, and finance and migrated to the United States at age thirty. He proceeded with advanced studies and earned a master of science in professional accounting (MSPA) plus certifications in certified public accountant (CPA) and chartered global management accountant (CGMA).

Rachi successfully served as an external/internal auditor, professor, and business analyst.

To properly progress in his newfound profession, he sought change of immigration status to Kenyan-American citizenship. The change enabled sponsorship of immediate family members and a few close relatives into the United States. Also, the new status opened doors of opportunity and allowed him to join and serve in the prestigious Federal Government's civil service. He served in this capacity for fifteen years until January 2018 when he officially retired from active duty at age 75.

Following retirement, Rachi founded the Village Food Bank Foundation, Inc., a nonprofit public organization of which he is the CEO and the managing director. The organization assists low-income minority populations with nutritional and basic economic and health needs in the urban towns of Prince Georges County, Maryland, and his native rural surroundings in Kenya. From a personal perspective, he enjoys the voluntary role of helping other human beings by caring and sharing his blessings with the needy—without regard to color, creed, sex orientation, nationality, etc. Rachi sincerely believes that God created all human beings equally and that his Spirit is common among human race.

Back in 2005, a vision occurred to him that he had the potential to write a lifetime story about himself and his family's legacy. Up until that time, he was looking for signs that the Lord was with him to provide the needed courage, strength, wisdom, the peace of mind, and the opportunity to get the project up and running. When he disclosed the intent of writing layers of his life story bit by bit, the family unanimously applauded, "It's about time!"

Rachi feels that the Lord has spoken. Almost fifteen years of facts gathering and recollections have resulted in the finished composition of jot downs. Having experienced seventy-seven earthly years of a mixed grill of his active past life, he is telling the world what it was like, how it was, what it has been, and what the future might hold. So here we go with Rachi's finished component of "been there, done that" initiative. Truly, this is an additional layer of the Ngaines family legacy. Enjoy it!

www.ingramcontent.com/pod-product-compliance
Lightning Source LLC
Chambersburg PA
CBHW031513120626
46545CB00005B/1863